The Verified Nobody's Brief Guide to Personal Finance

J. Corthell

Frugal Ink

Disclaimers

- (advice, how-to)

The author has made every effort to ensure the accuracy of the information within this book was correct at the time of publication. The author does not assume and hereby disclaims any liability to any party for any loss, damage, or disruption caused by errors or omissions, whether such errors or omissions result from accident, negligence, or any other cause.

This book is presented solely for educational and entertainment purposes. The author and publisher are not offering it as legal, accounting, financial, or other professional services advice. While best efforts have been used in preparing this book, the author and publisher make no representations or warranties of any kind and assume no liabilities of any kind with respect to the accuracy or completeness of the contents and specifically disclaim any implied warranties of merchantability or fitness of use for a particular purpose. Neither the author nor the publisher shall be held liable or responsible to any person or entity with respect to any loss or incidental or consequential damages caused, or alleged to have been caused, directly or indirectly, by the information contained herein. Every company and household is different and the advice and strategies contained herein may not be suitable for your situation. Any use of this information is at your own risk. You are responsible for your own choices, actions, and results.

Copyright

Introduction

Why should you care about personal finance?

"At the end of the day, if you're wasting your time by not investing in yourself, you're going to waste away- and that would be the greatest waste of all." -Richie Norton

The price of financial freedom is far less than the price of financial servitude: serving credit cards, loans, and other masters.

Imagine that you could simply answer the phone because it's likely a friend instead of a debt collector.

Imagine no longer fighting with your significant other over who spent what and when.

Imagine no longer feeling the stress of your debts weighing you down.

Imagine your student loans being gone and no longer a source of stress.

Finally, imagine being in a position to pay your bills and even splurge on yourself when you've retired from work.

If any of these things sound like fun or like more fun than you're having right now, you should care about personal finance.

Additionally, having something in place to deal with job uncertainty can improve your quality of life tremendously and give you the freedom to stand up for yourself in the workplace- if you have the money to take care of yourself, your boss won't be in a position to push you around and have you stand for it.

This book was made for people who want some financial coaching but can't afford a coach. It starts with the basics of savings accounts and budgeting, moves through debt, spending less, workplace benefits, investments, and the various tax-advantaged investment accounts available in the United States.

Okay, here's a simile for you. Your finances are like a dog. Now, I love dogs. You may or may not love dogs. Let's compare:

Dogs	Finances
Lovable and helpful	Helpful (numbers dorks like me find them lovable)
You have to pick up after them	Yeah, pretty much the same
Will lick your face if you let them	Will not lick your face, and you're barred from the accountant's office from now on
If you don't feed a dog regularly, it will grow sick, feeble, and die (and you're really cruel)	If you don't feed your accounts (put money into them), you won't have much to help you when you are sick or feeble
If you don't take care of a dog, it can bite you when you expect it least	Emergencies and unexpected problems happen. What kind of awful terms do you have to agree to in order to solve the issue? Paying 23% interest?
If you train the dog, that training can provide years of enjoyment and enrich your life	Being disciplined with your finances will make your life simpler. "I'll just transfer this money over," instead of, "To save money, I will eat peanut butter sandwiches for the next 3 weeks and hope that I don't get scurvy."[1]
If you care for that dog, the dog can save your life	"This emergency sure does suck. Thankfully I have something saved up for just this occasion."
Can save your kids from a fire	Can get you a hotel room after a fire[2]

---

[1] I knew someone who got scurvy on that kind of diet. Get your vitamin C!

[2] If your dog can make hotel reservations, your dog is amazing and I want to meet them. You can come too.

If you can think of some analogies to your favorite pet, go for it; I don't think this works as well for cats, birds, fish, or any other pet that's less than impressed with its owner.

The goal is for you to be relieved of your current debt-related stress, have a healthier relationship with money, and not be among the people who have nothing saved and would have to go into debt to cover a minor emergency ($500 or less).[3] You can go be stressed about your job and not having enough money but go home and have a full refrigerator (well, full enough). You can just go home and hug your spouse instead of holding a grudge about who bought the too-expensive couch. The cost is that you have to be disciplined about budgeting, sticking to the budget, and saving your money every month.

Anything worth having requires hard work. Anything worth keeping requires maintenance.

---

[3] Aimee Picchi, "A $500 surprise expense would put most Americans into debt," CNN.com, January 12, 2017.
http://www.cbsnews.com/news/most-americans-cant-afford-a-500-emergency-expense/

Chapter 1

Financial basics

"What people don't realize is that professionals are sensational because of the fundamentals." -Barry Larkin

Financial basics are important because you can't ever get to the important stuff if you're still fumbling on the basics. If you're in heavy debt and don't know how you'll get out, welcome! Getting you out of debt and ready to be free is an important part of the book.

The basics of finance involve some math (just algebra, no worries):

$$(Income - expenses) > 0 = happier$$

Or, as put in the Charles Dickens novel *David Copperfield*:

"Annual income twenty pounds, annual expenditure nineteen nineteen and six, result happiness. Annual income twenty pounds, annual expenditure twenty pounds ought and six, result misery."

Simple, right? Well, not easy, but simple. There is an army (or several armies) of people trying to get you to buy products with loans (e.g., credit cards, mortgages, car loans). Why? Is it that they want to level the playing field and have you live 'like the rich' do?

Well, no. They do it because it makes them money. Interest on debt is a powerful force and comes in every month like clockwork if people pay their bills. Most people do pay their bills, but have little left over for anything else.

This army makes it difficult to save any money. We also now live in an age where we get targeted advertisements at any time of day, and those armies of people with loans are trying to discover new ways to get targeted advertisements to you all the time.

So how do we combat this onslaught of advertisements, which are developed with the help of different experts to make these appeal to you as much as possible?

We can do it through budgeting and taking as much money out of our hands as possible.

That probably wasn't the answer you expected. However, we (as human beings) are pretty bad at resisting temptation and long-term planning, so we are going to send our money to the places it needs to go immediately. The basis for this plan can be illustrated with the following example:

If someone asks you for five dollars, is it easier to say no when you have the five and don't want to give it or is it easier when you don't have the five on you?

The plan is to move money around and quickly get more distance between you and your money. Basically, you will have different savings accounts (or 'buckets,' if your bank offers something like that) for different kinds of expenses and set money to automatically move to those accounts soon after your paycheck hits. We don't do these transfers immediately when your paycheck hits so that if you are laid off, you have some time to cancel those transfers. I'll have an example later in this chapter.

As a side note, here is some quick financial and life advice: whenever you are signing something, always read the fine print. It doesn't matter if it's making everyone else uncomfortable. Read the fine print. The 'gotcha' clauses, where you pay lots of extra money that you didn't realize you were being asked to pay or have to pay extra under really common scenarios, are always in the fine print.

Never go to a bank or meet an attorney without your reading glasses.

Make sure that you understand something before you sign it.

Bank account types and CDs

This will likely be very basic (i.e., unnecessary to read) for some of you. However, I know that there are many who have no idea what the differences are between the different kinds of bank accounts, so this is for you.

Savings, checking, and money market accounts and CDs

Savings accounts can be very basic. Read the fine print, of course, but generally the bank will let you keep money in a savings account in exchange for receiving some interest. Banks that you can physically go to, nicknamed brick-and-mortar banks, have much lower interest rates these days (below 1%, even below 0.1%), but online-only banks, if you're comfortable with that, offer interest rates of 1% and above. You can't write checks from a savings account; generally, you can get the money out via debit cards, ATMs, electronic transfers, bill pay programs, and bank tellers in the physical bank.

Savings accounts may also have minimum balances that you have to keep in the account, so watch out for that- the small fees that can be charged for having a balance below the minimum can eat away at your savings.

Savings accounts aren't for investing, they're for holding. Repeat this as necessary. Your money won't be lost in a savings account (aside from inflation[4]), but, in general, it won't grow at any rate that's worthwhile. There are savings/checking accounts with higher interest rates, but they generally have multiple hoops to jump through (e.g., 12 charges per month of at least $10 each, must check the website x times per month, must use our credit card, etc.). If you can deal with the requirements and want to go through the hoops, they are helpful, but they're not for everyone.

Checking accounts let you write checks. Many do not give any interest; those that do generally have either hoops to jump through (similar to the savings accounts) or have a low interest rate (like 0.25%). You generally want a checking account that doesn't have a minimum balance and doesn't have fees for writing checks or keeping money in there; generating interest is a definite plus, but if you can't meet the requirements for the interest, having the other two is still a good deal.

Money market accounts (sometimes abbreviated as MMAs)[5] are similar to savings accounts but have more significant requirements. You will need to keep a higher minimum balance, may be limited

---

[4] Inflation is a decline in the purchasing power of money (what a given unit of money can buy, e.g., how much candy can you get for 1 US dollar today compared to 10 years ago?) and an increase in what things cost. It's generally a small percentage each year, like 1-4%.
[5] Sadly, these are not nearly as entertaining as mixed martial arts.

in how often you can access the money, and banks can delay transfers of the funds in money market accounts (banks won't do this often, but they are legally allowed to do so). In exchange, you get a higher interest rate[6] and can write checks from the account.

Certificates of deposit (CDs) are loans you make to the bank in exchange for a given interest rate, a given rate of compounding (i.e., interest will be added every so often), and a given time frame, like 2 years (similar to bonds, which are discussed later in this book). CDs can be a little more flexible than bonds in that you can break the CD early to get at your money; however, you will have to pay an early withdrawal penalty (often abbreviated as EWP) of some of the interest if you break the CD early. CDs are generally considered very safe investments if the bank is FDIC insured.

Account type	Interest?	Can I write checks?	Must leave money there?
Savings	Yes	No	Only to meet a minimum
Checking	Sometimes	Yes	Only to meet a minimum
Money market	Yes	Sometimes	Only to meet a minimum
Certificate of deposit (CD)	Yes	No	Yes, for the term of the CD (e.g., 5 years)

---

[6] Well, *relatively* higher. The jump from, for example, 0.35% to 0.85% won't make you wealthy.

FDIC insured? What does that mean?

The Federal Deposit Insurance Corporation, or FDIC on almost all your bank paperwork, is a US government entity that insures your bank deposits for up to $250,000. This means that you can keep up to $250,000 in a FDIC-insured bank account (per owner, so if you have a joint account with someone, that is insured for up to $500,000[7]) and if that bank fails or goes bankrupt, the government will give you up to $250,000 of the money you lost, though there are no requirements for them to be timely about it. This is why CDs and bank accounts are generally considered safe, low-yield savings vehicles- the government insures them, so you're only out of luck if the government itself goes down[8] or the FDIC is eliminated.[9] Credit unions are insured in a similar manner by the National Credit Union Administration (NCUA).

Picking a bank

Picking a bank shouldn't take up too much of your time. You are looking for something that is convenient for you and meets your needs. You need to write checks and have few to no interruptions to getting your paycheck; if that's all you want, many banks and credit unions will meet those needs. Maybe I want something that is available everywhere; perhaps a nationwide or online bank will meet those needs.

---

[7] FDIC, "How Are My Deposit Accounts Insured by the FDIC?" https://www.fdic.gov/deposit/covered/categories.html, accessed in May 2017.
[8] In which case our fiat money no longer exists and the preppers will get the last laugh.
[9] Which is politically unpalatable; not impossible, but almost everyone likes the FDIC and how they stabilize banks.

Banks vs. credit unions

A credit union is a nonprofit organization that, in theory, gives its members better rates for banking transactions (car loans, interest, fees, etc.) but is generally localized to a geographic area or a specific interest group (a credit union only for teachers, for example).

A bank is a for-profit organization that is more widespread and open to any customers that meet their minimum requirements (for example, $10 to open an account).

Generally, a credit union will give you a better deal on some things (like loans) but is only open to a select group of people (though some credit unions are open to all, making them non-profit banks, essentially) and can't travel with you when and if you get a job in a new place or change professions (though this is changing more and more as banks increase their online presence). For example, if you belong to a teacher's credit union and switch careers from education to running your own bakery, you may not be allowed to be part of that credit union anymore and must switch to a different bank or credit union. Maybe you're part of the university credit union as a student and you get a job elsewhere- you may need to switch banks because you're no longer a part of that university.[10]

I didn't find it much of a hassle to switch banks when needed, so I stuck with credit unions. If you find it to be too much of a hassle, then use a national bank when in school (since you'll nearly inevitably need to move).

---

[10] This is generally not a problem if you use online-only banks; however, for online-only banks, there is no branch to walk into or relationships to form since you can't physically be there.

Interest rates

Interest: a proportion (usually a percentage) of the loan that is charged to the person receiving the loan as payment for the privilege of borrowing or using the money.

You generally want the highest interest rate that you can reasonably get; some banks will offer much higher than normal interest rates if you fulfill certain requirements, and average-to-poor interest rates if you don't.[11] If those requirements are too onerous, skip that bank and find one that offers interest rates that won't hassle you too much. Today's interest rates aren't that good,[12] and so they won't really give your money a chance to grow.

Savings accounts aren't for investing, they're for holding. Repeat this as necessary.

Online banks give better interest rates and are FDIC insured, so they have some appeal. If you're uncomfortable with a bank that you can't physically walk into, don't use online banks- it's that simple, and you aren't missing out on much. The really important part is to have something in savings and invest money to make those savings worth something.

Bank signing bonuses

There are websites and blogs solely devoted to finding the best bank signing bonuses, which are bonuses (free money) that you get in exchange for trying out a new bank or opening an account and

---

[11] For example, 3% if you meet the requirements and 0.01% for when you don't.

[12] Actually, they're terrible. The bank is lending your money at 3-30% interest and giving you 0.1% interest, if you're lucky, so from your $100 they get $3-30 and you get $0.10-if you left your money in there for a whole year without touching it in any way.

fulfilling some requirements, like taking on their bank credit card or leaving $5000 in the account for a full year. If this is something that appeals to you, you can spend a few hours a month jumping your money from place to place to get those bonuses (which, generally, you get in addition to the advertised interest for that account at that particular bank). However, read the fine print- maybe you have to leave it parked in that bank for 6 months at 0.01% interest and you'd be better off not switching. Maybe there are fees for closing the account or for not having direct deposits into that account (perhaps 12 transactions per month). Additionally, the minimum deposits may be too much for where you're at in your financial life; for example, there may be an offer for a $400 bonus, which sounds great, but you need a minimum deposit of $25,000, and you don't have $25,000 just lying around that you can leave there for 6 months. If you find a bank that you want to use anyway (it meets your needs) and you get some free money for going there, then do it and enjoy the cash when it arrives.

I personally prefer simplicity, and moving my cash around every 3-6 months, instituting up to 12 small debits per month for different accounts, holding an extra $10,000 out of investments (or even $100,000 to get all the bonuses I could) so that I can move it around into different accounts, and evaluating whether the money is worth getting my credit report pulled up multiple times, all in order to make an extra $500-2000 a year, isn't as worthwhile to me (I can earn more than that with my side job). Your situation may be different, and it may be a great deal. Just know that you can make some money by switching accounts and that it can eat up your free time.[13]

---

[13] There is a point at which your time is worth more than the money and vice versa- if you have the cash lying around, you can get an extra 1-2%

Interest compounding and compound interest

As you look through different bank offers, you will see an interest rate and you will see how often that interest compounds. This can lead to the phenomenon of compound interest. So let's start with the definitions:

Interest accrual: how often interest accrues (is calculated) for the account.

Interest compounding: how often the bank actually adds the interest to your account.

Compound interest: your interest starts earning interest.

As an example, let's say that you have an account that you are told accrues interest daily and compounds monthly. In this example, you get $0.13 of interest per day (interest accrual) for a 30-day month. At the end of the month, $3.90 is deposited into your account (interest compounding). The additional money deposited into your account as interest increases the amount of next month's interest, which still accrues daily (let's say $0.14). So the next month, you earn $4.20, 30 cents of which is compound interest ($3.90 is interest on your initial deposit, and $0.30 is your interest earning interest).

The importance of budgeting

Budgeting is important maintenance for your finances, though getting it up and running requires some hard work. This is where we start including automation.

Between credit cards, debit cards, one-click ordering, and autopay, it is really easy to not know how much money is in your account at

---

per year from such bonuses, but that may not really affect your overall financial situation.

any given time and how much you need to keep in there to avoid having any checks or payments bounce.[14,15]

You should know what you have available since banks charge a fee for every time you have insufficient funds to pay a check; therefore, every bouncing check suddenly becomes another fee for you to pay, and such fees can eat a whole paycheck.[16] It does feel a little ridiculous, though- as the comedian Gallagher noted, they are charging you more of what they know you don't have!

Budgeting is making a plan for your money. If you have a significant other that you share accounts with, you have to do this with them. I know that may sound like getting a root canal right after you ran over the dentist's cat,[17] but hear me out. If you want a plan that actually means something, as in you both stick to it, the other person involved with the money needs to be on board and you need to make sure that you're on board with the plan as well. If only one of you sticks to the plan, it's a bad plan. If both of you can do it, it's a better plan (so long as it isn't the old standby of "no planning, no savings, and let's hope for the best").

---

[14] *Bounce*: verb; slang meaning the check will not be honored by the bank because there wasn't enough money in the account to cover the cost. Banks charge fees for every bounced check.
[15] If I remember right, Mad Magazine joked that the classic movie *Casablanca* was really a movie about Bouncing Czechs. I'll be here all week.
[16] I also knew someone that lost a whole paycheck to bank fees.
[17] "Do you want to put the patient under anesthesia?" "No. Corporal Mittens didn't get any anesthesia, and neither do they." *Whirrrrr...*

Budgeting methods

Let's kick it old-school. Do you still have your old handheld calculator? The one that you had to use in school before smartphones all had calculators on them? No, just me?

All right, now that I've dated myself, get yourself a pen and paper. Amazingly, other than information, this is all you need. You don't even need the calculator if you can add; the calculator is just there to check your work and make things go faster.

We're going to start with two things: your balance sheet and your monthly budget.

For your balance sheet, write out your outstanding debts and the value of anything you might own, even if the answer is "nothing." Your car, if you've got one, has some value. My collection of Giant Microbes™ has some minimal value,[18] so it's not as important as the car. Treat the money you owe (outstanding debts) as negative numbers.

If you add the numbers together, it's a very rough approximation of your net worth. If it's negative, that's okay, we have to start from somewhere (and with student loans, there's a good bet that it's negative). This gives you a real idea of where you're at. This can be hard to look at, but admitting/realizing that there is a problem is the first step toward solving that problem.[19]

---

[18] This minimal value is called Garage Sale Value by those in the know; it basically means the item has as little or as much value as you can haggle for it, and so you're not likely to get even $5 for each item.
[19] Some clichés are repeated because they're true.

For your budget, write out all the bills and expenses you have in a given month and your monthly income. Write out all the expenses you have throughout the year as well- for example, if you pay $1200 per year for car insurance, once per year, then include $100 per month for car insurance (you can save that money all year so that the bill doesn't scare you when it arrives; this is also called a sinking fund).

Do you make anything over your monthly expenses? That is what you can start saving.

There are a number of apps and programs that you can use to help write out your budget. If you're a fan of spreadsheets, you can use them. The actual mechanism doesn't matter- the most important parts of a budget are 1) having a budget and 2) actually sticking with that budget.

The importance of saving first and sinking funds

> *"It's not the daily increase but daily decrease. The height of cultivation always runs to simplicity." -Bruce Lee*

It's important to save money first because it's really easy to *say* that you'll save whatever is left at the end of the month and then not have anything left at the end of the month. If you save first, then it's done, you don't have to think about it, and anything left at the end of the month is gravy; decrease the number of things you have to think about (see Bruce Lee quote above) and automate savings. Automatic savings and investment increase the likelihood of actually saving the money; one study showed that automatic savings increased the enrolled group's savings to over four times what the control group saved.[20] Automatic savings is recommended by behavioral economists, the American Psychological Association, and me (for what that's worth).

Therefore...

Automation Is Your Friend

If you are eligible for some employer-based automatic savings plan (direct deposit into an investment account, for example), that will help. Banks offer such plans already for your savings account and investment accounts offer them too. There are also interesting apps like Acorns (I have no relationship with them) that round up your purchases to save little bits of money at a time and invest it. You will have to do the budget to determine what you can save without any (or many) tears, but you can send that away to go be saved without you seeing it. Out of sight, out of mind, and not being spent on something you won't remember 3 days from now.

The research also shows that slowly increasing your savings rate in an automated plan further increases your savings because, once again, you didn't see it in your checking account to know that you put it away. If you can use automated savings, do it, and remember that automated savings is preferable to automated billing- because the outflow can disappear without you knowing in just the same way, and you definitely want to monitor the outflow; for example, if your power bill doubled this month, you want to know about that so you can start looking for the problem, instead of getting auto-billed and not knowing that the problem exists. If the costs are fixed each month, then auto-billing is fine (and may make things easier on you).

---

[20] Ashraf et al., "Tying Odysseus to the Mast: Evidence From a Commitment Savings Product in the Philippines." Q J Econ 2006: 635-672.

We'll discuss this in more detail later, but I advocate automated savings into some type of investment (e.g., retirement or brokerage) account instead of a savings account earning 0.05%; you want the money to do something other than earn you a bright, shiny penny per month.

Sinking funds are a great way to decrease the number of emergencies since fewer things take you by surprise. Sinking funds can be savings accounts or 'buckets' that have a designated purpose. The money goes from your checking account to these savings accounts after payday in order to cover expenses that come up every so often. An example might help, so see this table:

Account purpose or name	Amount moved each month
Property taxes	$200
Car insurance	$178
Car repairs	$60
Clothing budget	$40
Spend-on-myself money	$50
Vacation fund	$100

As the money is moved each month, it will slowly build up and you won't be left searching when, for example, a car repair bill comes up out of nowhere.

You need an emergency fund

"That which can go wrong, will go wrong." -Murphy's Law

Emergency funds go by many names. My dad called it Mad Money, your grandmother might have called it the rainy day fund, my good buddy calls his the Oh S**t! Money. This is for when something you couldn't or didn't predict goes wrong.

I am indeed a fan and believer in Murphy's Law. Your car will break down at some point (see the second law of thermodynamics), the weather will knock out your power lines and your heat during the winter,[21] a car will hit you after you just used up all your sick days, and many more. Just having some money on hand, waiting in some easily-called-up accounts, can help you sleep better at night and help your significant other sleep much better at night. If leaving your money somewhere can buy you peace of mind and let you easily sleep at night, was it worth it? I think the answer is a resounding yes; personal finance is personal, and more than just a set of numbers on a spreadsheet.

What is an emergency? Your situation may be different than mine, but I'll give a couple of examples that might help:

---

[21] That was a fun couple of weeks.

Emergency	Not Emergency
You lost your job and don't have another way to pay your bills	Your favorite doodads or clothes are 5% off
Your car breaks down, and it's the only way you can get to your job	Your car has lost that new-car smell[22]
You fall and break your arm, and need $5000 for the insurance deductible	Your local store is running out of the latest and greatest smartphones *for at least two whole weeks*!
Your house is destroyed by a tornado and you would like to sleep in some form of shelter tonight, thank you	You want a new deck, and yours has been rotting for years

Generally, if it's a big expense that you knew about well ahead of time, it's not an emergency; use a sinking fund instead.

The amount that you put in an emergency fund will vary by your situation and what makes you and the significant other (if you have one) comfortable. I consider the baseline to be at least 6 months of expenses (not what I make per month, but expenses, i.e., the bare minimum needed to live; if I don't have a job, I'm not going out for cappuccinos or dinner unless someone else is covering it). Why 6 months? Well, 6 months provides a better buffer for finding a job than 3 months and 9 months to a year's worth of expenses just takes a long time to get to (unless you've got a really good

---

[22] And that lovin' feeling.

income). My spouse feels much better with 6 months of emergency funding than 3 months. If your job is painfully secure, then you can work with a 3-month emergency fund, but I don't have that level of confidence, myself.

Some people state that you should not have any sort of emergency fund. Typically, they will tell you all about it using terms like "cash drag," referring to how savings accounts don't keep up with inflation (if your savings account will give you 0.10% interest and inflation is 2% per year, then you're losing real purchasing power[23]) . You should also note what these people say they would do in the event of a real emergency and determine if you're likely to do those things (you can also see if there's a difference between what they say to do and what they actually do). I'll give some examples:

1. "I would sell some of my investments from my brokerage fund."

If you're reading this book, it's likely that you don't have a 6-figure taxable investment fund (and a five-figure fund could run out in 1-3 months, depending on what you have saved). Neither do I. Therefore, this advice doesn't really help you at all. For grins, let's just say that you have something in an investment fund that you could sell. If you lost your job because the economy had troubles, then your investments are down as well, and there's the psychological factor of cementing in that loss by selling when things are down. Will you sell and keep the loss? Will you keep the

---

[23] This is a real phenomenon, but it may not be a real problem for you if you're more concerned about the emergency than whether your money is getting every last cent of value extracted from it. I want to be able to handle the emergency more than I want to worry about every last bit of investment growth. Plus, the other safe options suck.

money in the investments and hope that things go up while you just go without? Or will you take on debt and make a bad situation worse? This can be a viable plan, but that's likely much later in life and not right now.

Also, it should be noted that some investments, like mutual funds, may have rules that prevent you from selling repeatedly in a given period, which means that two emergencies or issues in a row would force you to find another source of money to deal with the problem.

2. "I would put everything on my credit card for the month and pay it off by getting money from [insert source here, e.g., Mom, Dad, investments, shady street operators, etc.]."

This is something that *could* work out just fine, but I'm not a fan. To start, debt is not cash- there is no negotiating, you owe interest if you're late, you need to find the money to pay it back, most people don't walk around with credit card readers,[24] etc. Additionally, credit card debt has higher interest rates than other forms of debt (except for the street operators and payday loans, but I'm repeating myself). If the emergency is a big one and the source of the money doesn't come through, then your 0%-just-borrowing-the-money becomes a loan with a 16-28% interest rate, depending on your credit card.[25] Payday loans are even worse; don't get a payday loan. Payday loans will only extend and multiply your misery.

---

[24] And don't go asking people where you can swipe your card on their bodies.
[25] I once had a 0% interest credit card that went up to 23% interest as soon as the card had a single late payment. Some of you are noting that it must have been a *good* card because it didn't go up to 37%.

So, taking things together, that money had better come through for this plan to work; otherwise, you've just made it worse for yourself by having no income AND a month's worth of expenses at 16-28% interest. Let's see what happens to that month's worth of expenses at 16% if you can't pay it for the next 6 months and, magically, don't add any more to it in those 6 months:

Month	Interest on $3000 at 16% per year	Total Interest
1	$40.26	$40.26
2	$40.80	$81.06
3	$41.35	$122.40
4	$41.90	$164.31
5	$42.46	$206.77
6	$43.03	$249.80

Now, you get a job in 6 months and things are looking a little better. Except now, with the lower rate of 16% interest, you can only pay the minimum of $200, which will get this paid off in...over 17 months. You won't get anything else for that money, it's just debt. Now, this is a rosy picture. Many people have been unemployed longer than 6 months. And if the debt is your only way to pay for things, then you'd have to take on additional debt each month. And that looks like...

Month	You Owe	Interest	Balance
1	$3,000.00	$40.26	$3,040.26
2	$3,000.00	$81.06	$6,121.32
3	$3,000.00	$122.40	$9,243.72
4	$3,000.00	$164.31	$12,408.03
5	$3,000.00	$206.77	$15,614.80
6	$3,000.00	$249.80	$18,864.60

Compound interest works for you in your investments and against you in any debt you have.

3. "I would just get a HELOC (home equity line of credit)."

If you don't have a house, this plan can't work for you. If you do have a house, know that the lender can pull your equity line right out from under you (reduce, freeze, or cancel it) if:
- Your home's value significantly decreases;[26]
- You miss your payment or pay late;
- You get a divorce and the spouse's income was necessary to make the payments;
- You can't afford the payments any more for some other reason;

---

[26] Remember when the US housing bubble burst in 2006-2012? Well, the bank remembers, and banks did exactly this- they canceled, froze, or decreased HELOCs because they were worried about going bankrupt themselves. Yes, it can happen to you too.

- You move out;
- Or you take another mortgage out on the house.

Additionally, many HELOCs come with variable interest rates, which can make things go from bad to worse if the interest rate is increased at a terrible time.

Also, if you lose your job because the economy tanks, that could affect the appraised value of your house, so the equity line goes poof.[27] If you have an emergency and can't pay your bills, that equity line can go poof. If you and your spouse have fights over money, the most common thing for couples to fight about, and your spouse leaves, the equity line can go poof.

I'm a very big fan of having the money on hand to deal with an emergency, and I don't like going out and applying for loans when I have just run out of money.[28]

4. "I can just depend on my spouse's income."

Not a bad plan, but it doesn't work for situations where you and your spouse lose income; if your spouse doesn't have a job, then this can't be part of your plan at all. This plan also doesn't work if you're single; it's also a bad idea to get married in a hurry because you're broke.

---

[27] It's a technical term. Think of a magician disappearing in a puff of smoke. Think of ninjas doing that if stage magicians aren't your thing.
[28] Bank underwriters are also not convinced to lend you money when you have no obvious way of paying it back. See the entire history of asking for co-signers on loans.

5. "I'll just take it out of my Roth IRA/401k (retirement plan), since I can take part of that without any penalty at all or pay it back as a loan."

Do many people advocate this? Yes. Do I think it misses the point of having a retirement fund (discussed later)? Yes. If you're going to raid your retirement plan for an emergency now, you forfeit all the gains and benefits of the investments; after all, you can't put that money back in all at once if you take it out (IRAs have a hard limit of $6000 per year that you can put in, as of this writing, so an $11,000 emergency would take 2 years to put back into the account). It's much better to just have an emergency fund.

Okay, let's say that you understand where I'm coming from, but you actually have oodles of money lying around in accessible places and you are concerned about cash drag.[29] You don't want an emergency fund. If you are one of those folks, then you just need to form an emergency *plan*. Your plan should include: where you would get money from that doesn't involve making a bad situation worse; things that you would actually do- closing out underperforming investments or the business that puts bread on the table are really bad options for your plan if you wouldn't actually do them; and ideas that don't completely wreck your plans for the future.

Or maybe you want an emergency fund but you're concerned a little about inflation. You can make a tiered emergency fund, but don't get too risky- investing is not the point of the emergency fund.

---

[29] Cash drag, definition 2: "my money isn't earning as much in interest at the bank as it would invested in [insert thing I think is better]."

A tiered emergency fund simply has multiple levels of savings. It's a calculated risk- generally, most emergencies don't need the entire 6 months' worth of savings (or however much you have) all at once. Tier-ing the fund allows you to have pretty safe investments or savings accounts (covered in the next section) but pays some attention to interest rates.

Perhaps this will be better illustrated through an example. Let's say that you a) have a 9-month emergency fund and b) have a spouse. Your spouse wants at least a month's worth of savings in a brick-and-mortar bank because they feel more comfortable being able to walk into a bank for at least some of the money. You have an online bank with better interest rates and better CDs. You can break the CDs at any time and lose out on some interest, but otherwise you'd get your money back in an emergency. That could look like this:

Tier	Physical bank	Online Bank	CDs
1	1 month of savings at 0.05%		
2		2 months of savings at 1.1%	
3			6 months of savings at 2.05%

You can configure your tiers how you like, but you get the idea: you can get better interest rates on your savings, it's still immediately available if you get into trouble, and these are safe options insured by the FDIC.

Some people like to use bonds or bond-based mutual funds (covered later) for a tiered emergency fund, but those are a little less safe and a little less easily available (also called liquid) than these options covered here. Just don't go overboard- the emergency fund is supposed to be money kept in safe places that can be accessed very quickly in an emergency. If you decide to throw all of your emergency fund into the stock market one week, the market can tank just before you need the money.[30]

---

[30] Don't worry, I'm not a psychic, just a firm believer in Murphy's Law.

Chapter 2

Debt

Credit cards (and signing bonuses) can get you in trouble

"Caveat emptor." -Latin for "let the buyer beware"

Hopefully, you were warned to not sign up for every single free t-shirt that you were offered in college, specifically because you were actually signing up for a credit card and got a t-shirt in exchange. I've seen salespeople offer t-shirts, 3-inch sandwiches, pens, and even hot sauce in exchange for signing up for a credit card.

The credit card is being given to you in the hope that you will incur some interest-bearing balance (i.e., don't pay off the whole bill in one month) and that it will cost you more than it cost the card issuer to pay that bill or give you the free goody bag.[31] For most people, this is a good bet for the issuer and they make money. At the time of writing, the market value of Visa stock is over $350 *billion*- they are making money.

That's it. That's how this works. I avoid using credit cards because I don't like owing anyone (I've always been that way) and interest can bite you if you're not aware.[32] If you can't bear to have that

---

[31] For the mathematically inclined: $220 interest > $1.50 per mass-produced shirt.

[32] As an example, look at how much of your student loan payment (if you have one) is going toward interest and not the principal each month. You can then do the math to see when they are making a profit off of you, i.e., if you borrowed $40,000, when would the interest + principal

kind of life (if you're thinking, "No credit card?! Are you some kind of Luddite or an Amish escapee[33]?"), then here's some advice about credit cards:

1. Read the fine print. Always read the fine print. What will you be charged for and when?

2. Determine the interest rate and calculate what you will have to pay on something if you just pay the minimum payment. Don't actually pay only the minimum payment; this is just so that you are aware of how badly you'll be treated if you make only the minimum payments.

3. Pay off the total balance at the end of each month to avoid paying interest. Autopay makes this easier at the possible cost of making you less aware of how much you're spending on the card.

4. Know what makes the interest rate change (late payment, holding a balance, etc.) and how much it changes (e.g., from 0% to 28%).

5. Know the fees for having the card. Yes, many credit card issuers will charge you every year for the privilege of having the card.

6. Understand the protections that are available for this card and those that aren't (e.g., what do I have to pay if someone steals the card and uses it).

7. If you are offered a higher credit limit, it means that the credit card company thinks they'll make more money off of you this way. They aren't making a judgment call about your trustworthiness or value as a human being.

---

you've paid exceed $40,000? At a $250/month payment and a 4% interest loan, it would be around year 13. Since most student loans are for 30 years and most people don't pay them off early, that's 17 years where the money is just gravy (roughly $51,000).

[33] Absolutely not. Both groups have much better beards than I do.

8. Actually use the reward points on your card. Most people earn credit card points but never use them, which is just like never earning the points at all.

As many wiser people have said before me, There Ain't No Such Thing As A Free Lunch (TANSTAAFL). You are being given a credit card so that a third party[34] can make money off your everyday (or larger) purchases.

But credit cards offer me better protection against fraud than my alternatives!

Depending on the issuer, debit cards can offer a lot of the same protections (and do particularly if you run the debit card as 'credit' since that runs the transaction through the card issuer's system), and some credit cards do offer more protections against fraud and identity theft; for example, you could be out $0 with a credit card up to a maximum of $500 with a debit card. However, you are also more likely to spend more on a credit card[35] and have the ability to carry a higher balance than you might normally keep in your checking account at any given time. The average person with a credit card has over $15,000 in credit card debt; do you keep $15,000 in your checking account?

---

[34] The three parties are you, the person or company you're buying something from (e.g., buying coffee from Starbucks), and now the credit card company (which collects a fee for its use).
[35] Soman, D. Marketing Letters (2003) 14: 173. doi:10.1023/A:1027444717586; Raghubit and Srivastava, "Monopoly money: The effect of payment coupling and form on spending behavior." Journal of Experimental Psychology: Applied, Vol 14(3), Sep 2008, 213-225. http://dx.doi.org/10.1037/1076-898X.14.3.213

TANSTAAFL. You (may) get better protections in exchange for a greater likelihood of spending more money and making others money.

If you are among the few who have the discipline to avoid spending any more than you would with cash or debit, pay off the balance every month, and use the rewards points, then congratulations: you're a rarity. For most of us, not having a credit card (and subsequently a balance) is far wiser. However, before you get too smug, run the numbers yourself and see if you're actually spending less.

Why do I suggest paying off debt?

Paying off your debts (credit cards, mortgages, car loans, etc.) is a wise move because paying off those debts will increase the amount of money that you can save each month for retirement investing, emergency funds, a down payment on a house (if you want one), or something else that you may want. Paying off debt increases cash flow and decreases the real amount that you pay for things; for example, $1000 on a credit card at 22% interest, if left alone, would bring the total cost to $1220. Finally, paying off debt relieves stress. Student loans suck. I want you to have hope of getting rid of the student loan one day.

Additionally, every dollar has a possible alternative use. For credit cards in particular, there isn't really an investment option available to you that would generate more interest than the card costs you (12-37% interest), so there's no alternative investment that will generate more money than paying off that debt.

Some people advocate using low-interest debt (like 3-4% interest) to invest because the history of the stock market has included returns above 6%; however, if the bill is due and your investments didn't work out like you planned (yes, people lose money in the stock market too), you get to a) pay for it another way, b) sell the investments at a loss and find other sources of the money, or c) declare bankruptcy and deal with other types of heartache. I prefer the simplicity and certainty of just having no debt; your tolerance may vary.

Paying off your debt

Your paycheck may only leave you enough to survive. To generate the extra money needed to pay something off, you may need to:

- Sell some of your things (books you no longer read, textbooks that are still in use (just not by you), old clothes, and more) in exchange for cash (not gift cards or the like, which you can't use to pay off the debt);
- Take on additional work or responsibilities, like working extra hours if possible, taking on additional part-time work, selling a service that you can provide,[36] etc.;
- Lower your monthly bills in order to make room for paying off your debts, e.g., changing your cell phone plan to have an extra $20 in your budget.

Your debt has two components: the interest and the principal. The principal is the actual amount you borrowed and the interest is the extra money you are being charged for the privilege of having the loan. For example, let's say you have a $1000 credit card debt at 16% interest[37] with a $40 minimum payment. You pay it on time

---

[36] I offered tutoring services for years.
[37] Which is a lower rate than the overall average as of this writing (19%, according to ValuePenguin.com).

(66 months, or 5.5 years) and end up paying $1396.70 in total for that debt (assuming that you didn't add anything extra).

Principal: $1000
Interest rate: 16%
Interest: $396.70

Over time, you essentially overpaid for the stuff by almost 40% and it probably didn't last you 66 months. Additionally, debt adds stress to your life, your marriage, your job (if your debt is bad enough, you may have to keep a job you hate to make all your payments), and especially any bouts of un- or underemployment.

As such, to simplify your life, I recommend that you pay off your debts and avoid taking on more of them- life is too short to have personal financial stresses overtake your life.

Your debt payoff plan: snowball or avalanche?

There are three main ways that you can pay off your debts, two of which I recommend:

1. **The "debt snowball" method**: while making the minimum payments, pay off the smallest debt first (in terms of monetary value, i.e., pay off the $50 loan before the $100 loan, no matter what the interest rate is), and use the additional money that is no longer being used to pay off the previous debt to pay off the next smallest debt, moving onward until every debt is paid off;

2. **The "debt avalanche" method**: while making the minimum payments, pay off the loan with the largest interest rate first, i.e., pay off the $2000 loan at 5% interest before paying off the $50 loan at 3% interest, and use the

additional money that is no longer being used to pay off the previous debt to pay off the next-largest interest rate, moving onward until every debt is paid off; and

3. **The "unwavering optimism" method**: pay off your debt haphazardly (no strategy, just throw extra money at something each month) and hope for the best.

I recommend methods 1 and 2 and don't recommend 3; without a plan, you won't know when you've made progress and you will lose your motivation. To make this above clearer, let's look at an example.

In this example, you have 4 sources of debt with different interest rates and a little extra money that you've discovered due to your own diligence.[38] You have:

1. A $15,000 car loan at 3% interest for 5 years, with a minimum monthly payment of $270;
2. A $1,000 credit card debt at 16% interest, with a minimum monthly payment of $40;
3. A $2,000 credit card debt at 21% interest, with a minimum monthly payment of $80;
4. A $25,000 student loan at 4.5% interest for 30 years, with a minimum monthly payment of $126.67.
5. An extra $150 each month to pay off your debts.[39]

To start, your monthly payment for the debt is $516.67 per month,[40] of which around $179 is just interest. Let's look at a comparison of the snowball and avalanche methods.

---

[38] Good job! Diligence pays off.
[39] If you can't even get this much extra per month, that's fine; you just need to get something in order to get started.

Snowball method

Debt	Monthly payment	Debt is paid off in...	New amount you can use for next debt
$1000 credit card	$40 ($26.67 goes to principal)+$150	6 months	$190 per month ($150+40)
$2000 credit card (now $1744.73)[41]	$80 ($45 goes to principal)+$190	Additional 8 months	$270 per month ($190+80)
$15,000 car loan (now $11,938)	$270 ($240 goes to principal)+$270	Additional 24 months	$540 ($270+270)
$25,000 student loan (now $23,568)	$126.67 ($33 goes to principal)+$540	Additional 36 months	Done! Now $656.67 can be saved each month.

With this plan, your debt is now paid off in a little over 6 years (which will be tough, trust me), but you'll be debt-free and have saved about $16,474 in interest over making the minimum payments forever (remember, the total debt was $43,000, so you saved enough interest to pay for 38% of the total value).

---

[40] For comparison, when I started working, I made $1200 a month.
[41] In this example, it is now $1744.73 because you've been paying the minimums and not adding more debt.

Avalanche method

Debt	Monthly payment	Debt is paid off in...	New amount you can use for next debt
$2000 credit card	$80 ($45 goes to principal)+$150	11 months	$230
$1000 credit card (now $706.63)	$40 (26.67 goes to principal)+$230	Additional 3 months	$270
$25,000 student loan (now $24,538)	$126.67 ($33 goes to principal)+$270	Additional 62 months	$396.67
$15,000 car loan	$270 ($240 goes to principal)...paid off at 60 months	Paid off already	Added to student loan payoff when car was paid off

With this plan, your debt is paid off around a little over 6 years, you'll be debt-free, and have saved $16,728 in interest over making the minimum payments forever.

Comparison: snowball vs. avalanche method

In the last section, I showed you an example of how you would pay off debts using the two methods. The avalanche method saved $254 in interest over the snowball method (your numbers will obviously differ). So which is the best?

Whichever one you will actually follow through on.[42]

The debt avalanche method gives you better numbers (in the example, the avalanche method did save us more money, and depending on your debts, it could be a lot more money).

The debt snowball method works better for your motivation and mindset.

If you are disciplined enough to follow the avalanche method, it will give you better numbers (i.e., pay less in total interest), but I recommend the snowball just because it gives you peace of mind earlier. For instance, in the example case we just covered, the first debt is paid off at either 6 (snowball) or 10 months (avalanche); would you lose sight of the goal around month 8 if you didn't have any noticeable success? Getting rid of the smaller stuff helps you to stay motivated, and motivation is one of the keys to getting control of your finances.

The best debt payoff plan is the one you'll actually see through to the end.

Now, imagine what it would be like to live without any debt. You own your home. You own your cars. You don't owe anyone any money and can spend and give much more freely since you aren't worried about debt.

If you need motivation, make a wish list. Write down the top 30 things you would do if you didn't have any debts. What would you spend your time doing? Would you look for different work? Would you take a (deserved) vacation? Would you give more of your time

---

[42] I say the same thing about working out and dieting.

or money? Write down the top 30 things you would do if your life were free from debt and refer to that list when things get rough.

Chapter 3

Lowering your bills

"When your outgo exceeds your income, the upshot may be your downfall." -Paul Harvey

If you're just starting out, you don't have too many bills to lower, but you should still watch out for places that you could be getting a raw deal. Here are a couple of saving strategies to get you started (there is room for creativity, but don't do anything illegal).

Cut out the clutter from your budget

There are two ways to approach this. For the first method, you can find cheaper sources of the things that you want/need. For example, at least once a year you should look to see if someone will offer you a better deal on car insurance and internet service. Are you able to put some services together for a cheaper deal? Don't be afraid to ask for a better deal; some companies will find a way to work with you if you'll stay as a customer. See if some of your fixed costs can be cut or decreased in some way. For example, I have known some people to switch internet providers each year so that they can stay at the 'new customer' rate.

For the second method, you can cut out the things that don't matter to you. For example, I don't watch much television at all. What television I do want to watch is available by using an antenna or can be streamed via the internet. So I cut out cable television. That's around $50 a month that I can put toward the things that I do care about- that's a decent dinner date, a couple of drinks at the bar (with tip, of course), 12 mornings of cappuccinos, or a new pair of on-sale shoes. If you don't really care about something, why are you paying for it?

Roommates and housing

If you're a student, it is nearly universally a bad idea to buy a house. You lose all the flexibility of moving when a job opens up because you'd likely be left paying both a mortgage and the rent on the new place. You also likely don't have anything near a decent salary, which makes it hard to be 6 figures in debt. Finally, most students will need to move out of their college town in order to pursue permanent employment, so you're likely not going to stay in that one college town forever and you'll need to offload that house before you can completely leave.[43]

If you have a decent job and are looking to stay in the area, a good rule of thumb for the size of a house or mortgage is that the house (or condo) should cost (total) 2-3 times your annual income. Do the calculations to see if you can pay the extra costs (taxes, maintenance) every month in addition to the mortgage or cost of saving up for the house. If your house costs more than 3 times what you make in a year, you'll have a hard time saving money for retirement and investments and will also likely have a hard time making property tax payments and keeping enough money around for maintenance. Shop around for mortgages- the best bargaining position is one where you can walk away from a bad deal. Finally, if you do this, you should save up some of the money you were previously spending on rent to account for house-related expenses (if the roof collapses, you're the one left with the responsibility).

---

[43] Or become a long-distance landlord, which is really hard if you're working at the same time.

If you're a student, you likely should have roommates. Renting out a room or having roommates can also be very helpful for paying off your mortgage if you own the house. If you find a good group of colleagues or friends, getting a shared apartment or house can work out well. For many people, food and housing are the two biggest items per month that eat up the budget. Finding roommates, finding people who want to sublet their garage,[44] and other creative ideas can help decrease this big expense.

You also can live outside the immediate vicinity of your workplace. You can still find deals that have easy commutes that are outside the area and therefore cost much less to rent.[45] Being willing to look and look early will help you find the deals if you can't find any roommates.

Groceries

You need to eat, despite what some people believe. You'll have to spend some money on groceries, which are also cheaper than total food replacement options, like having meal-replacement shakes and those alone (not that I recommend those options; I find that the sensation of taste is quite enjoyable). Here are a couple of ways to save on groceries, some obvious, some not.

Sales

Now, the usual advice applies: buying stuff on sale works well if you're going to be using the item quickly (I can buy chicken on sale if I'm going to cook it within the week; if I expect it to last a month, that probably won't work), have a freezer, or the item isn't going to go bad quickly (or at all). Stores have clearance racks

---

[44] Make sure that the door locks, though.
[45] I did rent a place that cost 40% of what a comparable apartment near the school would have cost. It was close enough that I biked into work.

with perfectly good things that just didn't sell in that store, for whatever reason. I've found very popular name brands (and treats!) in those racks at 75% off because no one wanted them where I lived.

Coupons

We live in a time where it's much easier to clip coupons than in the past. You used to need to cut coupons from the newspaper and save them until it was time to use them. You can now load coupons onto your grocery store card and they will be automatically applied at the speed of your click. These are typically the exact same coupons offered in the newspaper, so you don't have to cut those anymore (though you may have to cut some).

Absorb that for a moment- you have instantaneous savings because you were willing to click. How many times a day do you click with a mouse? How many times do you click for something less valuable, like cat GIFs?

If you need to save money, clipping coupons for things you actually buy is kind of a no-brainer. Most of the big stores in the US will accept competitor coupons as well, and you can get some great deals on things that don't go bad (quickly) by doing this.

Pooling groceries

If you have roommates, you're probably already doing this to an extent. However, let's get creative. Perhaps you and a friend have a fondness for rice but each of you only has $4 that you can put toward the rice. Rice is one thing that gets cheaper as you buy more of it. If you pool your $8, you can get more rice than you would get for $4 and split the package. Now you can save the extra rice for the future.[46]

You can also go in with friends on a warehouse store membership (think Sam's Club or Costco); for items that don't spoil, these stores provide pretty good deals (25 pounds of dry rice will last you quite a while when you're single).

If you have roommates, pooling groceries just makes sense. Unless you have individual refrigerators with padlocks, then it doesn't seem useful to try to separate the fridge into "my stuff," "roommate 1's stuff," and "roommate 2's stuff."[47]

Slow cookers

A slow cooker is my friend. It made my neighbors jealous on many nights that I returned from work after 7pm.[48] It can be your friend, too. Slow cooker cookbooks abound, and you can find many recipes that require you to a) dump stuff into a slow cooker, b) turn on slow cooker (make sure it doesn't have a bunch of exposed wiring; that's not a good slow cooker), and c) walk away. This may not be gourmet stuff, but if you're on a tight budget, then this home-cooked meal is a lot cheaper than the stuff in the freezer section and better than going hungry.

But where can I get recipes for slow cooker meals? Well, you have access to an entire internet. Additionally, if you don't have internet access, then you can go down to your local library (they still exist). You can also get cookbooks there if you're willing to do the arduous task of returning them. You can also feed a whole group

---

[46] Or gorge yourself on carbohydrate goodness.
[47] "And the stuff that Chris' girlfriend leaves here."
[48] "Your house smells delicious. It's smelled delicious all day. ...I'm sorry if that sounds creepy."

of people if they're willing to throw some cash your way for the meal.

Libraries

Books, movies, audio, and internet access. All these things are available at your local library (there's even more at many university libraries if you have access). Do you want a DVD or Blu-Ray movie? They're at the library. Books, audiobooks, and music CDs are at the library. You can sit at the computers and use the internet to find the different things you're looking for.

You don't even have to pay for a library card. That's a pretty sweet deal.

DIY

You probably need to fix your own car. If you don't have a lot of money rolling in, then maintaining the car is important. If you don't have any experience with this, then find a friend who does.[49] They'll likely have some tools to help you and can at least get you going on a basic job, like changing your oil or checking your battery.

There are likely other repairs and maintenance that will fall on your shoulders. Enjoy it- some of this stuff can be fun and you'll end with the satisfaction of knowing that the thing works because of your effort.

---

[49] Full disclosure: I was that friend for a couple of people. As Red Green said, "If the women don't find you handsome, they should at least find you handy."

Sometimes opportunities arise. I helped people move on a regular basis. When I did that, I didn't ask for compensation (you're just helping a friend, right?), but people would offer me things so that they didn't have to pack them or move them around. I've received furniture, lots of food, cleaning supplies, pots and pans, and a rug this way.

I had a friend who would collect fish for his experiments. The extras had to be disposed of, and so he offered to bring them over if I would get him a steak and prepare the food myself. I invited people over and told them to bring something- I was out grilling for 10-20 people (happily) and usually had plenty of grilled fish left over, which was more expensive food than I could afford at the time. It was always a great time.

I've filled out surveys for gift cards and combined gift cards in order to get someone a nice birthday gift. I tutored students for pay and as a volunteer. I gave product reviews in exchange for gift cards (always honest ones). I kept an ear out for opportunities to do something extra (like this book[50]).

If you are willing to look for opportunities, they will come. Keep your eyes open and be willing to work a little (or a lot, as the case may be[51]).

---

[50] Note: most books don't make any money, but they are fun to write.
[51] I remember helping someone move their grand piano. After hours of mistreatment, tempers were about to flare when my spouse showed up with beer and pizza, saving the day without knowing it.

Chapter 4

Benefits are important

"You don't know what you've got 'til it's gone." -Joni Mitchell, "Big Yellow Taxi"

Workplace benefits are crucial if you can get them. Benefits will come out of your paycheck, but they will vastly increase your quality of life. This will be US-centric; my apologies to my non-US readers.

Health insurance

Health insurance is the big benefit and the most obvious benefit; many people lament not being able to just go to see a doctor when they are sick. If you can get on a group plan, you should; the uncertainty in the US health insurance market has made it expensive to get your own plan. Even after subsidies, I have been offered plans that cost more per month than I was paid per month. Any sort of group benefit through your workplace is likely to be cheaper and more comprehensive than what you can get on your own.

Here are the things that are worth checking out in your health insurance plan (in short, the whole thing):
- Co-pays (the amount that you will pay, as your share, at the doctor's office or the pharmacy for your prescriptions)
- Deductibles (how much will have to come out of your pocket before the insurance company starts to pick up the tab?)

- Is the deductible high enough to qualify you for a health savings account (HSA)? For single people, the minimum deductible is $1300 per year and is $2600 for families in 2017.
- Out-of-pocket maximums (how much will you be asked to pay in total for your whole family per year?)
- Benefit maximums (how much will the insurance company pay in one year? This is more of an issue with chronic illnesses)
- What procedures are covered? Are you expected to pay to visit a specialist?

If you plan on having children during your time at that particular workplace, check what kind of maternity coverage they have. Paying for all maternity care out of pocket isn't fun.

Dental insurance

You should get dental work done, period.[52] Dental insurance, however, should be looked at with a skeptical eye. Most dental insurance covers 50% of the costs of dental work, which can often mean that you're spending more on having the coverage than you're getting out of it. If your coverage will cover more, then just be sure that you're not paying too much for it. For example, if your insurance only covers tooth cleaning, a cleaning costs $75, you get two cleanings a year ($150 total), and you pay $30 a month for it ($360 per year), you are overpaying unless you get some other benefit.

---

[52] A good friend of mine went without dental checkups until their tooth abscessed and they were in tremendous pain. The root canal and associated surgeries cost more than the cost of all the missed cleanings.

When I had no dental insurance, I still saved the money to get at least two cleanings per year. That office cut me a deal because I paid the whole balance off in one check and the dentist's office didn't have to go through the hassle of dealing with an insurance company.

Vision insurance

Vision insurance can have the same pitfalls as dental insurance if you're dealing with glasses; I keep pairs of glasses for years, so that benefit only comes up once in a while, and the cost of visiting the optometrist might not be that high. If you get contact lenses, though, the cost of your insurance covering it could work out quite well for you.

Most vision insurance does not cover laser surgery to get rid of your glasses. It should be noted, however, that the rate at which your vision gets worse seems to plateau around age 50, so if you get laser surgery at 25, you will likely need it again later. Also, if you have astigmatism, laser surgery may not work on your eyes (at least with current technology).

Life insurance

"Insurance is the only gamble where you lose if you win and you win if you lose." -Mad Magazine

I have a family. I have a young family that would be in a lot of trouble if I suddenly died. As such, I do keep life insurance and I got it as soon as my first child was born. Some workplaces offer life insurance as a benefit; I signed up for the benefit, but it was still too meager to take care of my family if I died. As such, I signed up for another plan outside of work.

Life insurance is a benefit that is paid out if and when you die during the terms of the life insurance contract. If I die young (while I'm covered by the insurance), then my surviving family will receive some money to help them pay the bills and survive.

Any life insurance is legalized gambling; when I buy a life insurance policy, I am gambling that I will die within the specified timeframe and will pay much less than the insurance company will pay out, while the insurance company is gambling that I will survive the term and they will take all the money as profit.

The types of life insurance currently available are:
- Term
- Increasing term
- Decreasing term
- Permanent
  - Whole life
  - Universal life
  - Variable
  - Variable universal
- Survivorship
- Final expense (aka burial or funeral insurance)

Term life insurance is good because it's simple to understand and cheap; if the premiums are paid and the insured person dies, the agreed-upon amount of money will be paid to the beneficiaries (the people who get the money; in my case, my wife and children) if it happens within the term (5, 10, 15, or 20 years or so). Term life insurance is cheap, effective, and does what it says on the tin. If you keep renewing these as you get older, they will get more expensive.

Increasing term life insurance means that the payoff amount increases as time goes on, whereas decreasing term life insurance means that the payoff decreases as you get older (but the payments likely won't change).

Permanent insurance doesn't have a term but instead goes on until the insured person dies. Most permanent plans have some sort of savings or investing side, but it's usually a losing proposition for you; if your surviving spouse (or other beneficiary) gets the agreed-upon payoff amount but none of the savings or investments, they are usually losing out. Alternatively, they can just get the savings or investment component, which may be less than what you thought was the payoff amount.

Whole life involves a savings component that can grow over time and eventually, possibly provide dividends to you, but the savings grows at a rate that is set by and benefits the insurance company, not you.

Universal allows you to have more control over where the payment money goes (your benefits or your savings), but remember that you don't set the interest rate on that savings account.

Variable and variable universal are similar to whole life and universal except that you can invest in stocks, bonds, and the like instead of just the savings account. Typically, the insurance company gets the biggest share of any benefit that your investments produce.

Survivorship insurance involves multiple people and can vary by when the payoff actually occurs. It may pay out when person 1 dies or when person 2 dies.

Final expense insurance can be quite useful for someone in a bad situation, like a prepaid funeral. If you're taking care of an ailing parent who doesn't have a pair of nickels to scrape together, prepaying the funeral or having a way to do so can be very helpful-those grieving don't have to find the money to pay for things. As someone who has needed to find a way to cover an unexpected funeral,[53] it can be pretty stressful to find the money (in your accounts and any you've been given authority over) to pay for the funeral that is happening in 2-3 days in addition to trying to grieve, clean things up, get all the legal paperwork done, and comfort others who are grieving.

I prefer and strongly suggest simplicity- in this case, term life insurance. Who benefits when you combine your life insurance with a savings or investment plan? The insurance company, typically. Let your savings be your savings and your life insurance be your life insurance. I have not yet seen one of these Franken-plans that try to be two things at once succeed at doing either thing well.

---

[53] Though I suppose that an expected funeral is the kind of thing that lands someone in prison...

Insurance type	Description	Recommended?
Term life	Pays specified amount when person dies	Yes
Increasing term	Payoff amount increases with time	No
Decreasing term	Payoff amount decreases with time	No
Whole life	Combines insurance with savings	No
Universal life	Combines insurance with savings	No
Variable	Combines insurance with investments	No
Variable universal	Combines insurance with investments	No
Survivorship	Pays when specified people die	No
Final expenses	Pre-pays funerals and related costs	Maybe

Retirement plans

Retirement plans will be covered thoroughly in chapter 6, but I do suggest seeing where and what your employer contributes. If they contribute to your retirement plan, contribute what you need to contribute to get the full match- a 5% contribution is like getting a 5% raise without a promotion. Just remember that you want to invest in stocks, bonds, and things like that- annuities are only really useful when you're already retired.

Check what options you have at your workplace, and if they're really terrible, just contribute enough to get the free raise and put the rest of your investment money elsewhere.

Chapter 5

Things you can invest in, i.e., what on earth a stock is

"Invest we must." -John Bogle

The goal and purpose of investing is not to get rich (much less get rich quickly), but to avoid being poor in your old age.

You need to save for emergencies, and you need to save for retirement if you're in the US or the UK. Period, end of story. You don't want to be an old person eating pet food because it's the only thing you can afford.[54]

Investing is the practice of allocating some scarce resource (e.g., money, time[55]) toward something because you expect to get some benefit that is more valuable than what you put in. For example, you may pay money to invest in a stock because you expect to get more money out of it than you put in (either through dividend payments or the stock's price appreciating). You invest time and money into a relationship because you believe that the benefits (emotional, financial, etc.) are worth more than the time and money that the relationship requires. You likely invested time and money into your education because of the potential payoff! Interestingly, investment rules have been around since the Code of

---

[54] Felicia Lee, "Fear of Hunger Stalks Many Elderly," New York Times, November 16, 1993.
[55] Youth, innocence, and honesty are also scarce resources, but those are apparently easier to waste than to invest.

Hammurabi; the human trait of hoping to make lots of money[56] has apparently been around for a while.[57]

Why should you invest your money in stocks, bonds, real estate (including REITs),[58] and the like? These investments are among the few vehicles that will generally keep up with the cost of inflation and are widely available. For example, individually purchasing real estate (i.e., buying a house) will keep up with inflation,[59] but you're not going to start buying houses with $100 to your name. Hedge funds are huge, require lots of money to get involved with one, and you have to know where to go.

You (we, actually) have to beat inflation. Inflation has ranged in the past from 1-5% per year,[60] and therefore your investments, whatever they are, need to beat that in order to have any real growth (real growth is defined as growth beyond inflation, e.g., if inflation is 2% and your investment yields 3%, your real growth is 1%). It would be very hard to pay your 2020 bills with the amount of money that was considered a fortune in 1910. Also, it's hard to save up the money you need to all by your own power; you need something that grows or generates interest.

---

[56] Read as: greed. Insert Gordon Gekko references here.

[57] Since 1700 BC, baby! There's nothing like a classic.

[58] REITs = Real Estate Investment Trusts. Invented under the Eisenhower administration as a way for middle-class folks, as opposed to the rich alone, to invest in real estate.

[59] In terms of the cost of the house; if you're using the house as a rental, remember that the rent payments may pay for the overall cost of the house in 20 years or so, not immediately.

[60] In the United States. Source: US Bureau of Labor Statistics, CPI-All Urban Consumers, 2007-2016.

The goal and purpose of investing is not to get rich (much less get rich quickly), but to avoid being poor in your old age.

That's it. Investment (in the financial sense) is saving up money and buying partial or full ownership of something in the hopes of taking advantage of growth in value, compound interest, and/or dividend returns so that you can beat inflation, have your savings grow, and have it grow enough that when your body is tired and breaking down, you will have some sort of game plan for eating and keeping a roof over your head. That news story about old folks eating pet food? They were subsisting on Social Security alone. I'm not denigrating anyone who has to do that- I'm pointing out to you, the young(er), that subsisting on SS alone is really hard, unpleasant (to put it mildly), and not really what any of us imagine retirement is supposed to look like- no golf courses, exotic travel, or expensive hobbies are really feasible when you aren't able to eat.

Here are the five things you need to remember about investing for retirement (or for additional income):

1. You need to understand what you're investing in. If you don't understand it, either read up until you understand it or leave it alone. If you don't understand your investment, there's no real way you'll feel comfortable holding onto it if something bad happens (or be able to identify when that something bad happens).
2. You need to be comfortable with what you're investing in, or else you'll freak out as soon as things look a little bad and undo most of your gains. People typically get greedy and invest at market highs and then sell when things start to decrease, locking in the loss.[61]

3. Keep your costs low. Someone charging you 1-2% of your retirement funds every year greatly affects your gains.[62] Some groups will even charge you 5% or more, which really drags your investments' growth.
4. Time in the market (staying put and reinvesting the dividends/bond repayments) is more important than switching things or leaving every time you feel bad, feel angry, see something that everyone is investing in, someone suggests a new get-rich-quick scheme, you get a newsletter, or you get a sales call about investing in the latest fad.[63] Stick it out. Do not be scared by what the finance journalists or latest newsletters say.[64]
5. Automated saving is much, much better and easier than saving what's left over at the end of the month.

If you learn at least those five things, this book has been a success (well, at least this part of the book).

So what is the quote at the start of this chapter about? Well, it's to make sure that we all understand that this is not a get-rich-quick book or strategy. Yes, some people do really well by making big bets in the stock market. Most people who play the game get

---

[61] A recent example is the rise of Bitcoin and everyone and their brother jumping in...and its subsequent fall (not a crash, but the decrease was enough that I quit hearing about Bitcoin for a while).

[62] Full disclosure: currently, "keep costs low" = investing in index funds. However, I like and invest in index funds and think it's a great deal for *us*.

[63] Phone call 1: "There is no beef jerky left in the US! Buy jerky futures!" One week later: "I know that last week I said that beef jerky was in crisis, but we found a new supplier. The US is now running out of denim patches for fixing pants! Invest in denim patches!"

[64] As the joke goes, they've predicted 27 of the last 2 recessions...

burned, and so this book and this chapter are about *not playing the game*, i.e., I advocate the strategies that are really boring but also help you avoid getting burned.

I favor simplicity in my investments: I make sure that I understand them, that I understand what they are doing, and that my simple strategy is one that I can keep up with. The data appear to show that my simple strategy (which many other people share) is likely to beat out much more complex strategies.

All right, you're thinking about investing for your retirement in some way, shape, or form; so what do you invest in? We'll start by discussing what stocks, bonds, and REITs are, as well as a (brief) discussion about investments that fall outside of these categories, such as hedge funds, annuities, and commodities (and why they aren't part of the strategy that I recommend for you).

Stocks

You've likely heard of stocks already.[65] You may not know what they are, but if you've ever been near a newspaper or near some finance show while stuck in an airport or waiting room, you've heard of them.

A stock is a share of ownership in a company (which is why you may have heard of them as stock shares or heard stock described as shares). If the company makes a profit, you are entitled to a share of that profit; when that profit is distributed to you, it is called a dividend. Dividends are a significant portion of the total return you get for owning a stock; the price of the stock may not change, but

---

[65] No, not the medieval public torture device, though some people feel that way when watching financial news.

dividends are actual dollars and cents (or whatever currency you're using) given to you as your share of the profits. The other part of a stock's total return is the capital gain: if you sell the stock for more than you paid for it, the difference is called a capital gain (any investment, including a house, that you sell for more than you paid for it involves capital gains, because your money [i.e., your capital] paid for it). If you don't sell the investment, you don't have any capital gains (i.e., all of your gains might just exist on paper but not actually in your pocket).

Companies, it should be noted, provide dividends at their discretion. As a stock owner (shareholder), you are stuck with two sometimes-opposing desires: you want the business to do well and increase in value (to provide you more value for owning that stock) AND you want to get dividends on a regular basis (because that's cash in your hand). Therefore, if the profits are reinvested in the business (like buying some large piece of equipment, for example), it still benefits you in some way, but it may not benefit you immediately or as directly as getting a dividend would. I write all this to say that you are not guaranteed a dividend, many companies don't pay them out (they need to reinvest to help the business grow, particularly companies in the biotech, medical device, and pharmaceutical industries), and it might not be in the shareholders' best long-term interests for the company to give a dividend.

One should note that selling stock is one of the ways that a company can use to finance itself- bonds, also discussed in this chapter, are another way they could raise capital (i.e., money).

The value of owning a stock lies in 4 things (forgive me, finance majors, if I'm missing some minutiae):

1. How well the company is doing: is the company profitable? Are they selling something that people want?
2. The dividend returns: are they regular? Are they considerable?
3. Human emotion: is the company well known? Do people believe that this company is going to skyrocket in value, even if they don't actually have a product?[66] Do people believe that the size of this company's dividend is worth the extra cost to own it?
4. Inflation: the cost of a stock usually grows with inflation (though with considerable lag time), regardless of the other factors.

In my opinion, a lot of the overvaluation or undervaluation of stocks is likely in this 3rd portion, the human emotions surrounding that company. This is why different companies will get huge valuations before they even have a viable product to sell- profitability and dividends don't exist yet for that company (and so stability is not guaranteed either), leaving only the human emotion factor.

Owning a stock is inherently risky- no one can successfully divine the future (if you can, you've already bought the right stock, and TV psychics wouldn't perform on TV if they knew which stocks to buy). If the company that you own stock in does well, the stock price goes up, dividends are paid out, and you can:

- Use those dividends for your purposes (e.g., pay your bills);
- Reinvest them in either the same or a new venture;

---

[66] Don't laugh, this was basically the 1990s dot-com bubble. And Theranos.

- Sell the stock at the higher price and make some capital gains;
- Or keep the stock and hope it continues to grow in value.

Please note that, as we'll discuss later, taxable vs. tax-advantaged accounts make this a little more complicated.

If the company does well, the stock price increases and more people want to buy shares of that stock. If the company does not do well, the stock price goes down or becomes worthless (when the company no longer exists). For example, if you found a treasure trove where your grandfather left you a bunch of Eastern Airlines stock, you know how much it would be worth today?

$0. Eastern Airlines doesn't exist anymore. They went bankrupt and stopped existing in 1991.

"Well," you might say, "owning stocks sounds pretty risky since my entire investment can go up in flames!"

Yes, you are quite right; investment, as a whole, is risky. However, consider the alternatives.

- You could save all of your money under your mattress. Over the time it takes to get to retirement, inflation would have taken a lot of that value away. For example, $5 in January of 1970 is equivalent to... $32.94 in February of 2018. That money would have likely at least tracked inflation over that time if invested, and the stock market's track record is good *if the investment was held at least 15 years*.[67] That can be a high bar to clear, which is part of

why retirement accounts are such a nice invention (especially if you pay a penalty to remove the money early[68])
.

- You don't save anything at all and wait for Social Security or an equivalent to come in. Reminder: the folks eating dog food or choosing to starve certain days of the week were on Social Security alone. In previous generations, such people were either taken care of by their children or starved. This is a tough road and doesn't look like a fun retirement. It's far better to have Social Security pay for the bulk of your retirement and still have something extra to have a little fun.

- You could put it all into real estate. This can work out if you're lucky and you happen to have the money to purchase the real estate when you're young- real estate does keep up with inflation, typically, but doesn't always appreciate beyond that (except for housing bubbles). If you don't have that money when you're young, it doesn't have the ability to appreciate as much in value as other investments. You could also finance the whole thing with debt, but that is how many people have lost their entire life savings in real estate (if all the bills come due and you

---

[67] There's a caveat here; the data show that you wouldn't have lost the money you put in over 15 years (if you put in $5000, you'd have at least $5000 left), but doesn't guarantee that you'd match inflation (think of cashing out during a recession). Stocks are always risky, which is why the bonds section of this book exists. You need to include some bonds to protect yourself.

[68] The research appears to show that people are more averse to a loss than happy about a gain, which makes people more likely to mess with their retirement accounts when things are going badly. This means that the tax penalty (for taking money out of the retirement account before age 59.5) somewhat works in your favor-if it prevents you from raiding the account or taking everything out.

don't have the real money to cover it, you're out of luck). You may also buy in a housing bubble with inflated prices and have to sell when the prices have come crashing down.

When I consider the alternatives, I think that investing in the stock market is accessible to me and more likely to leave me fed in my old age. Back to the point: investing in *individual stocks* is very risky, but that is the very reason that mutual funds were invented.

Mutual funds

A mutual fund is a mutually funded[69] (get it?) collection of stocks. The manager of the fund chooses what stocks to buy, and you are paying for partial ownership of the fund (along with many other people, hence "mutual"), not the individual stocks themselves. Mutual funds eliminate some of the risk of stock ownership by spreading the risk by owning multiple unrelated stocks (diversifying), which is the primary means by which any investor can decrease their risk. Risk is used a lot in the financial literature, and it means the likelihood of a negative event, e.g., you lose all your money on bad stocks or your investments do poorly and you've still got money, but not enough to fully fund your retirement.

As an example of how mutual funds work, think of gambling on a horse race. In this particular race, you can win money if you've bet on any of the top 8 horses, with different odds for each place. There are 20 horses. Owning individual stocks is like betting on one horse- if that horse is in the top 8, you've made some money. If they're in the bottom 12, you've lost money. Diversification is

---

[69] Meaning that the money of everyone who invests in the fund is pooled together and your returns are for your share of the pooled investment money.

like betting on 10 horses- your hope is that more of the 10 you bet on end up with a podium finish so that you balance out the losers that were picked (and so you make more money than you put in, when all is said and done).

To stretch a metaphor, a mutual fund is where you give your betting money to a bookie who places bets on the 10 horses that <u>he</u> thinks will win.

An index fund is where you place bets on all 20 horses (this is an oversimplification, but you get the idea).

Now, where the metaphor breaks down is that in the stock market, all the companies you own a part of could make you money in a given year (or lose you money in a given year). You are hoping that the majority make you money (dividends, the part of the company's profits that they pay to people who own stock in their company) or increase in value (capital gains, the increase in the value of the stock from when you bought it to when you sell it) over the time that you own your stocks, and that this gain is enough to offset the losses from the duds that you owned.

Thankfully, this kind of logic worked for investors. Warren Buffett has opined, "Diversification is protection against ignorance; it makes little sense if you know what you are doing." I would argue that the data clearly show that most investors and managers don't know what they're doing (80% or so don't match the market average each year, and those that beat it each year aren't necessarily the same ones that beat it the next year or the years afterward), and therefore diversification works in our favor; we'll discuss this more in the section on active vs. passive strategies.

Exchange-traded funds (ETFs) and index funds

Both ETFs and index funds try to track a given index by owning all the parts of that index; for example, a S&P 500 index fund or ETF would try to own stock in every single company in the Standard & Poor's 500, the top 500 companies in the US, whereas a commodities index fund or ETF would try to own a selection of commodities so that their performance would match a selected commodities index. Index funds work more like mutual funds, whereas ETFs are traded like stocks. They have some differences in terms of fees and ownership requirements, but they are otherwise pretty similar for the purposes of our discussion.

Stocks and mutual funds are great in tax-advantaged retirement accounts (accounts that either let you pay taxes later on the investment or let you pay taxes now and don't pay taxes on the total growth, e.g., 401(k) plans, individual retirement arrangements (IRAs), and Roth versions of these), but they can also be good in taxable accounts; dividends are typically paid quarterly (and so you are only getting extra taxable income 4 times a year) and the majority of the gain is in the value, which decreases how often you pay a tax on the investment.[70]

Bonds

A bond is another way that a company or government can use to raise money. Just as there is a stock market with constant trading, there is a bond market.

A bond is a loan from you to another entity for a set amount at a set interest rate for a set amount of time. The value of the bond on the bond market depends on how creditworthy the borrower is (i.e.,

---

[70] Why yes, accountants *are* paid for good reason.

how likely are they to pay you back?) and the interest rate on the loan; you can gain or lose money by selling in the secondary bond market, which takes place after the loan is generated. If the borrower can pay you back and you reach the end of the loan time (maturity), then you are paid back the whole amount that you loaned them plus the interest. Depending on the terms of the loan, you may get the interest all at once at the end or throughout the term of the loan.

For example, let's say that I have a simple bond for which I paid $10,000 at 2% interest for 5 years:

Year	Interest	Total Principal	Total Interest	Balance
1	$200	$10,000.00	$200	$10,200
2	$200	$10,000.00	$400	$10,400
3	$200	$10,000.00	$600	$10,600
4	$200	$10,000.00	$800	$10,800
5	$200	$10,000.00	$1,000	$11,000

Because the bond's terms were set at the beginning of the agreement, the terms are not affected by how well or badly the economy is doing (though the person's ability to pay back might be!). As such, it is uncorrelated with the stocks you may own, and this can help you: if the stock market is crashing but all your borrowers are paying their loans on time (sometimes stock prices go down while the fundamentals of the businesses are fine, i.e., they are still profitably selling their products), you're still making some money and can weather the shock of the market crash better than someone who doesn't have that safety net.

Investing in bonds is typically easier to do through bond-based mutual funds (aka bond funds) rather than buying the individual bonds. Similar to stocks, buying bond funds spreads the risk of a borrower defaulting across many bonds and reduces the risk that you personally take. Bond funds typically consist of government bonds (highly rated and some lower-rated) and/or company bonds (high and low ratings here, too, but not rated as well as US government bonds). Some of these bonds, if they are unlikely to pay back the debt, are called junk bonds.

Overall, because bonds pay out interest every month, it is a good idea to put bonds or bond funds in tax-advantaged retirement accounts; any bond interest in a taxable account is going to be taxed like the income from your day job (which can really drag your returns if you, for example, only make 2% interest and 28% of that is taken out as taxes, leaving you with a growth of 1.44%).

Government bonds

These bonds are issued by federal, state, and local governments. Federal bonds (US government bonds) are considered the safest bonds and usually are considered the minimum investment value that you would compare against, as in the following example:

Let's say that federal bonds are making 2% interest. If the stock or mutual fund you are offered has the possibility of growing at 2%, then it's not worth investing in, because you could avoid all the risk inherent in owning stocks and get 2% growth in very safe federal bonds. If the stock or mutual fund has the possibility of growing at 7%, then it might be worth investing in the stock instead of investing your money in bonds to get the guaranteed 2%.

State and local governments (in the US) also issue bonds as a way of trying to pay for larger projects (or typical projects) that their tax income will not cover, like updating a sewer system.[71] These bonds can vary wildly in their quality and likelihood of actually getting paid back and typically are not rated as highly as federal government bonds, but are generally rated as highly or more highly than bonds from companies.

Company bonds

Companies also release bonds as a way to raise money. Companies are started and go bankrupt with some regularity (not always the same company, mind you[72]), and so these bonds are considered more risky than government bonds. They also can have correspondingly higher interest rates to compensate for the fact that they're risky. Some company bonds, if they're risky enough, are called junk bonds, though junk bonds are not just limited to companies.

High-yield (junk) bonds

A junk bond is a bond that has a high interest rate and a high likelihood that the borrower will fail to pay back the money (which is why the interest rate is so high- you may lose all your money).

---

[71] It's also harder to get monetary support from companies or wealthy folks for these projects; everyone wants their name on a college building ("The Herbie Derbie Building of Wicked Smaht Chemistry") versus a mundane building that references some of the ugly things in life ("The Sloot McGroot Poop Chute Sewer System").

[72] Like the old joke goes: "Did you know that someone is hit by a car every 30 seconds in New York?" "He must get awfully tired of that."

Buying a junk bond is a bet that the interest will be enough of a profit that, when they default, your loss will be minimal or that you will have no loss at all. If you invest in these bonds, you will benefit from diversification and spreading your risk by investing in junk bonds through mutual funds or ETFs.

Who sells so-called junk bonds? Well, the term 'junk' is applied by an outside party, typically one that determines the likelihood of paying back the loan (like Standard & Poor's or Moody's). Junk bonds are bonds from risky companies, counties, or even countries. The idea when someone buys a junk bond is that the interest rate is high enough to justify taking the risk that you won't get paid back. Because taking on a junk bond with a high interest rate (like 13%) from someone who likely doesn't have the money to pay it back feels like a foolish endeavor, I invest in these only through bond funds (if at all) in order to spread the risk, not directly buying the bond myself ($10,000 is hard to come by, period, much less $10k to just put in hoping that this time, *this time* Zimbabwe will pay it back in some meaningful way).[73]

Certificates of deposit (CDs)

As discussed earlier, a CD is basically a bond with a bank; you can also invest in CDs in your retirement accounts. The interest rates and terms (length of time that you must keep the money in the CD) of CDs can be comparable to those of government bonds (sometimes even better!), and CDs are insured by the FDIC, which means that CDs don't really carry any risk. For your retirement accounts, CDs are very low-risk, low-gain investments. When you

---

[73] From March to December 2007, Zimbabwe's inflation rate was 240%. By November 2008, it had risen to **79 billion percent**. If someone offers you a Zimbabwe bond at 15% interest, run away- you'll get your Zimbabwe money back, it'll just be worthless.

are investing, CDs can be used with bonds or in place of bonds (it doesn't have to be all one or the other), though be warned that *brokered* CDs (which may be available in your tax-advantaged accounts) generally have lower interest rates than what you can get if you search for CDs yourself.

That said, if you had a million dollars and put it into a 1-year CD at 2%, you'd get $20,000 in interest next year, and that could make for a really nice vacation or 5 hours in Vegas with a side of heartbreak. However, other investments could make you a lot more money than $20,000 or possibly lose some of your money (remember, all investing has some level of risk or some kind of risk).

Alternative investments

Real estate investment trusts (REITs)

Real estate investment trusts (REITs) are a kind of specialized stock that invests in real estate. REITs were initially created under the Eisenhower administration to allow people with much less starting capital (like me!) to invest in real estate. Many REITs actually own commercial real estate and collect rent every month. This is a way to invest in real estate without having to personally own the real estate, though the REIT charges fees to cover their overhead (people need to eat). A REIT needs to pay out 90% of its taxable income as dividends to its investors, which means that REITs, like bonds, pay out dividends on a regular basis (which, if the account is taxable, almost all of those dividends will be taxed like the income from your day job).

REITs typically grow faster than bonds but carry the same risks as stocks (these are companies, after all). Research supports the idea

79

that, over the long term, owning REITs is a good approximation of owning real estate, but they carry the same risks as investing does overall. There ain't no such thing as a free lunch.

REITs are an American invention, but interestingly enough, international REITs were recently invented and modeled after American REITs. International REITs invest in real estate companies outside of the US; these are good for diversification and may be much easier to invest in for those of you who don't live in the US.

REITs, like bonds, are good to have in tax-advantaged retirement accounts.

If you believe that owning real estate is a good idea for you but don't have the money to get started, REITs may be a good choice.

Hedge funds

Hedge funds are similar to mutual funds in that they are pooled investments with multiple parties; however, hedge funds use different methods to try to alleviate risk than those available to mutual funds and are not limited in how much debt they can take on (they can be run on much more debt than any mutual fund). Additionally, they are sold only to institutions (like universities) or accredited investors (which means people that already have a lot of money, like a $2,000,000-net-worth-or-more kind of money) and cannot legally be sold to the general public. They are out of my reach and likely out of your reach.

I don't like the terms that go along with investing in a hedge fund. Many hedge funds have a minimum percentage of the total assets that they will take in fees in addition to a percentage (e.g., 20%) of whatever gains are realized in the fund. A quick example:

Big Daddy Warbucks[74] invests $2,000,000 in a hedge fund with 3% of assets-under-management fees, a fee of 20% of growth, and the hedge fund's growth for the year is 8%.

Initial investment growing at 8%	Fees on initial investment	Fees on growth	Left
$2,000,000	$64,800	$32,000	$2,063,200

...for a total growth over the year of 3.16% instead of anything close to the 8% growth.

I view hedge funds as active investing on steroids and therefore they don't fit into my strategy (not that I have the money to be invited into one, you understand). If you don't understand what the investment is or how the money is being invested, leave it alone.

Commodities

Commodities investing means investing in what the future prices of a given good, a commodity, will be. To be considered a commodity means that the thing in question doesn't really vary substantially between the people that make it or grow it: you can't really tell the difference between bananas grown by farmer A and those grown by farmer B, so bananas are considered a commodity and you can't tell the difference between pure gold mined by company C versus pure gold mined by company D, and so the gold is considered a commodity. Examples of commodities: bananas, coffee beans, gold, silver, platinum, cherries, pears, apples, beef,

---

[74] From *Little Orphan Annie*.

pork, orange juice,[75] cotton, and iron. A commodity that is selling well right now can be called a hot commodity.[76]

A 'futures contract' is when someone agrees to buy or sell a given good at a specified price. For example, if you agreed to buy bananas at $0.05 per pound for a whole ton of bananas in year 1 and the actual price of bananas in year 2 (future, remember) is $0.10, then you can turn around and sell the bananas you bought at $0.05 for $0.10 and make money. Generally, commodities don't do well (or predictably) when stocks are doing well, and they appear to do very well (but no more predictably) when stocks are doing poorly (a recession or depression). Also, if you trade them, you need to sell the futures contract before the farmer/producer delivers them or...you will suddenly be responsible for physically handling that ton of bananas. I assume your apartment won't handle that well.[77] You'll also have the very real possibility of your ton of bananas rotting away while you look for a buyer.

The people who usually invest in commodities or futures contracts are the people who work with the thing in question; in the previous example, people who either grow bananas or sell banana smoothies would be interested in banana futures. There are also speculators, but that just means people who believe they know which way the price will go- and that is their day job.

---

[75] The climax of the movie *Trading Places* specifically involved orange juice futures.
[76] Though really attractive people have been referred to as "hot commodities," you likely can't (or shouldn't) invest in them as part of your retirement or savings strategy.
[77] Though you'll be in a great position to trade in fruit fly futures next year...

Since you're likely not personally involved in raising cattle, coffee beans, or bananas or drilling for oil, I don't suggest investing in commodities. If you're moonlighting as a farmer or spend your free time working on an oil derrick, then make sure that it's not more than 5% of your entire retirement savings- if the past is similar to the future, commodities investment will lose you money most years and work spectacularly in others (though those good years likely won't offset the bad years).

Annuities

An annuity is an insurance contract and a bet with an insurance company. The insurance company, in exchange for some lump sum, agrees to pay you $X per month or per year for the rest of your life. You are betting that you'll live long enough to get more than that out of the insurance company and they are betting that you'll die before you can recoup that lump sum.

For example, a company might offer you an annuity that will cost you $3,000,000 and will pay you $3000 per month until you die. That means that you must live longer than 1000 months (83.3 years) before you make more money than the insurance company was paid- that's a bad deal that can look really nice when you're desperate (though you shouldn't necessarily be desperate with $3,000,000 in the bank) or not looking at the numbers ($3000 per month is more than double the value of some people's Social Security checks). If you paid $300,000 for that contract, though, then you've done better in 8.3 years, which is just a little more manageable.

There are also investments called income annuities. These function like annuities but they don't necessarily send you the money (and so you don't pay taxes on these until the contract expires). They

83

have longer terms than many bonds and CDs (they can start at 5 years or 7 years) and higher interest rates because if the insurance company can't pay the bills, they won't pay for that annuity either (and there's nothing like FDIC insurance for this market).

Annuities can have their place when you are already retired; however, their rate of return is less than you would get with other investments. If you do not think you have the self-control to live off of your savings in your retirement, an annuity might be a good decision. However, just remember the following:

1. Annuities can be expensive. You'll have to have saved up a significant amount of money in order to pay for the annuity.
2. If the insurance company goes bankrupt, you're out of luck.
3. Don't buy into an annuity unless you're already retired; if your workplace retirement plan offers annuities, see if you can avoid investing in them until later.

Investment	Description	Recommended?
Stock	Partial ownership of a company	Via mutual funds or ETFs
Bond	Debt that someone owes you	Via mutual funds or ETFs
Mutual fund	A collection of stocks and/or bonds	Yes, but index funds are better
Index mutual fund	A mutual fund that buys all the stocks that make up an index	Yes
ETF	An index mutual fund that trades like a stock	Yes
CD	Debt that a bank owes you	Maybe
REIT	Partial ownership of a company that works with real estate	Maybe
Hedge fund	Like a mutual fund with more investment options and greater costs	No
Commodity	Farm products and futures	No
Annuity	Insurance contract for $X per month	In retirement
Target-date fund	Invests in mutual funds and adjusts to become less risky as you age	Yes

Chapter 6

Retirement investing: accounts and concerns

"Growing old is not an option. We don't have a choice. But we do have choices that will greatly affect our quality of life for the rest of our life." -Henry Hebeler

First: what is retirement?

Retirement is when you are no longer working for (hopefully) the rest of your life. You can retire at the point when you can *choose* to stop working. If you have enough money saved up that you can decide to never work again and all your bills will still be paid, you can retire and go do other things with your time. If you want to keep working, that's fine. If you want to go play golf in the Galapagos, that's fine. The essence of what we call retirement is being financially independent and making your own decisions about how to spend your precious time.

Since pension plans have (largely) gone the way of the dodo (i.e., extinct), saving for retirement in the US involves different plans that are given favorable status as far as income taxes go; these accounts are also called tax-advantaged accounts.

Tax-advantaged accounts (401(k), 403(b), 457(b), IRAs)

Briefly, a tax-advantaged account is an investment account that receives some sort of beneficial tax treatment. Here are the main two types in the US:

- Traditional 401(a), 401(k), 403(b), 457(b), and IRA plans: anything you contribute to a traditional retirement plan is deducted from your income for that year (so you pay less in taxes today) but any withdrawals (in 20-30 years) are taxed as income (like a day job).

- Roth 401(a), 401(k), 403(b), 457(b), and IRA plans: anything you contribute to a Roth 401(k) is considered part of your income for the year (i.e., no deduction, pay more in taxes than a traditional plan) but all withdrawals are tax-free.

One more time:

Traditional = pay no taxes now, pay taxes on the whole thing later
Roth = pay taxes now, don't pay taxes on the whole thing later

401(a) plans

Only non-profit employers (like universities or other schools, hospitals, or religious organizations) can offer 401(a) plans. These may not be voluntary and don't need to be offered to all employees. As such, these may or may not allow you to decide how the money will be invested. The contribution limit on a 401(a) plan ($55,000 per year in 2018) is not shared with any other plan.

401(k) and 403(b) plans

Most workplaces these days offer 401(k) or 403(b) plans (these are named after the section of the law that created them). 401(k) plans are for for-profit companies, and 403(b) plans are for non-profit groups.

You can contribute up to $19,500 per year into one of these plans from your paychecks and only from paychecks (as of 2020). If you have multiple jobs and you have both a 401(k) and a 403(b), that $19,500 is shared between your plans. Your employer (if you are eligible for benefits) can offer a match as an incentive. If you get a match, contribute at least up to the match; it's "free money."

Again, if the plan is a traditional plan, your taxable income is reduced by the amount you personally put in (not the employer match). If you are offered a Roth plan, then you pay taxes on what you earn but whatever the account grows into will not be taxed later (as far as income taxes are concerned). The plan type (traditional or Roth) as well as what investments are available to you depends on what your employer has negotiated with the investment company.

If you have low-cost mutual funds (especially index funds) in your plan, then it can be a very good thing to fill the account (all $19,500). If you are only offered okay investment options, then it can be good to fill up to the match (otherwise you're missing "free money"). If you are in a really high tax bracket, then it can be great to fill up to the max (IRAs have income-based limits on whether your contributions are tax-advantaged, whereas 401(k) and 403(b) plans do not).

If your plan only offers annuities and no other options, it may be better to forgo contributing to the plan; however, you can also go talk to the people who organized the plan and ask them if they can include some other options. If they say yes, you can contribute without worry. If they say no, you do have other options.

If you have savings from previous jobs, then you can do a rollover if you have a good plan to go to.

What on earth is a rollover?[78]

A rollover is when you combine the money from your old and new retirement plans into one plan (typically the one for the job you're at). For example:

- You saved money in your retirement plans at jobs 1 and 2.
- Now you are at job 3.
- If you like job 3's plan better than the plans for jobs 1 and 2, you can move your savings from the previous jobs' plans into your current job's plan.

If you have a good plan to roll your savings into, then it can be easier and simpler to have only one place to look at for your retirement savings. Rollovers are also a good idea to do immediately after changing jobs because the old workplace needs to verify that you left, and if the company ceases to exist, you have to cash out. You can always roll over to an IRA for maximum control (though this has a different name, it functions similarly to a roll over).

457(b) plans

457(b) plans are for government workers (state and local, which can include public universities) and some nonprofits. However, you should be very sure of which kind you're contributing to when you start: if you are eligible for a governmental 457(b), then it functions a lot like an additional 401(k), but if you are eligible for a private 457(b), I recommend that you avoid using it.

---

[78] Not to be confused with turnovers, which are delicious fruit-filled pastries.

If you are going to contribute to a 457(b), then you can contribute up to $19,500 a year to it, in addition to what you contributed to your 403(b), for a maximum of $39,000 a year. This, like the 401(k) and 403(b), may have traditional and Roth options, depending on your employer.

Governmental 457(b) plans are, after Orange County (CA) went bankrupt and lost part of the 457(b) assets,[79] now held in trust, per federal law. This means that if the state or county goes bankrupt, the money is held somewhere else and the creditors can't touch it. This is a crucial difference between the governmental and non-governmental plans; the money in a non-governmental non-profit's 457(b) accounts could be lost to creditors in a bankruptcy.

You can also withdraw money from a governmental 457(b) before age 55 without a tax penalty, unlike a 401(k)/403(b). However, it's still a bad idea to drain your retirement accounts before you need them.

Individual Retirement Arrangements (IRAs)

The humble IRA is something that is not offered by your employer; you need to go set it up yourself. The nice thing about it is the freedom; you can go pick and choose whoever you want to hold your IRA for you and pick from all of their available investment options. The downsides are the limited amount of savings you can put in each year and that no one is going to put a match in it for you.

---

[79] Floyd Norris, "ORANGE COUNTY'S BANKRUPTCY: THE OVERVIEW; Orange County Crisis Jolts Bond Market." *The New York Times*, published December 8, 1994.

You are limited to contributing $6000 per year across all of your IRA accounts; if you are married, your spouse needs to open up their own accounts and they can contribute $6000 to theirs. As such, a married couple (whether both are working or not) can contribute up to $12,000 per year to IRAs (2020 numbers).[80]

For IRAs, you can get a traditional or a Roth IRA (or both) if you so choose. The $6000 limit is across all accounts, so you could conceivably open up six IRAs (3 traditional, 3 Roth) with $1000 each for the year. It wouldn't really benefit you to do so, but you could.

Traditional vs. Roth- what do I choose for my retirement savings (contributions)?

Traditional means that you pay taxes later when you withdraw the money from the account in retirement (e.g., you put in $5000 this year and the IRS treats it as though you made $5000 less this year in income). You pay taxes on what you withdraw in retirement, so there's no figuring out what was a contribution and what is growth or dividends; you're taxed on everything you withdraw. There is a tax penalty (usually an extra 10% on the amount in addition to what you would pay in taxes anyway) if you withdraw it from the account before you are 59.5 years old.

Roth (named for Senator William Roth of Delaware for the law creating these accounts, first proposed in 1989) means that you pay taxes on your contributions now (e.g., so the $5000 you put in this year is treated by the IRS as taxable income if you earned it this year), but you pay nothing when you withdraw it in retirement.

---

[80] This is a legal thing, I'm not saying that you shouldn't share with each other.

There's a lot of strategy put around which of these you put money into. My rule of thumb, for what it's worth, is that if you are in the 12% tax bracket for income taxes (or whatever is lowest or next-to-lowest), Roths are a great deal. If you pay more than that in income taxes, you're likely saving more money by going the traditional route. Additionally, you can end up with more money overall if you use traditional plans and invest the tax savings, but many folks don't have the discipline to do so.

If you want to just pay the taxes now and get it over with, Roths are wonderful. You can do the calculations yourself to determine what will work best (save you more money), but the rule of thumb can help you make a quick decision.

Retirement Plan Options			
Plan name	Contribution limit (2020)	Type of employer	Employer Match?
401(a)	$57,000	Non-profit	Typically
401(k)	$19,500	For-profit	Typically
403(b)	$19,500	Non-profit	Typically
457(b)	$19,500	Non-profit	Not typically
IRA	$6000	Any kind	No

Concerns

If you want to invest in the stock market, some kind of mutual fund is likely to be your best bet, compared to owning individual stocks. You will be confronted with two real options that will determine what kind of products you get and how you treat them.

First choice: will you be an active or a passive investor?

Active means that you will be a stock trader: you will do short sales, buying the latest thing that you believe is hot hot hot, and actively working to make enough small gains that you will have significant gains by the end of the year (though you're not opposed to large gains). Frankly, will you really have the time for this? You might have kids, a spouse, pets, or any other responsibilities that take up your time.

Passive investing will likely be more your style. This is the classic buy-and-hold style that is described by John Bogle, Warren Buffett, and many other investment luminaries. You buy something (stocks, bonds, houses, condos, etc.) and hold onto it for a long time (or forever) to reap the dividends and hope that your investment grows in value. You have to be disciplined and not freak out and sell everything you own when the market is down or tanking. You buy the thing, and you hold it for a long time (for example, now until retirement; we're talking more than 15 years).

Okay, next question, where we'll start with stocks (choice 2): if you choose to invest in stocks, will you purchase individual stocks, shares of active mutual funds, or shares of passive mutual funds?

First off, this is not necessarily a forced choice; you can do all 3. I do want you to think about it, though.

Individual stocks are risky; hopefully I convinced you of that earlier. If you must, limit them to part of your overall investment plan (less than 5% of the money), and have the majority be in funds so that you can be somewhat diversified.

Passive mutual funds are index funds and ETFs. You own some portion of the whole market and you get the market return, minus costs. Costs include trading costs (the cost of buying or selling a stock or bond or fund share), the expense ratio (what you see on the fund's prospectus, or information sheet), and anything else hidden in the fine print; the point is that your costs are not just the expense ratio that you read about. If you don't trade a whole lot, your costs are reduced; passive funds are typically managed by computers and don't have human managers checking on them every day, and so their expense ratios are typically less than 0.2% of the total assets per year (meaning that 0.2% of your total assets will be taken out from your account as part of paying the bills).

Active mutual funds have a manager who is doing the work of being an active stock trader. They are the ones who are paid to look at company info sheets, value companies, and determine if it's worthwhile to get that stock or not. You get the return of the companies or investment vehicles that the manager chose, minus the costs. The manager expects to be paid for their time, as they should, which usually increases the expense ratio above that of index funds or ETFs. If your fund manager doesn't trade a whole lot, your costs are reduced. Their expense ratios plus miscellaneous expenses are usually 1-5% of the total assets per year.

Purchasing active funds is a gamble that the person managing the fund is able to pick enough winners that, <u>after costs</u>, you will beat the market average (the relevant index). Passive funds (index funds) are the gamble that, after costs, tracking the index will continue to work better than any active fund manager.

Therefore, you would decide to invest in active funds if you want the chance to beat the average market return at the expense of having a very real chance of not beating the market return.

So...why did I say that tracking the index would *continue* to work better?

History notes

Some recent scorecards have come out that point out a couple of things to note about the past. I should note, as every investment vehicle in our litigious culture notes, that the past is not indicative of anything that will come in the future. There are no guarantees in life other than death and that someone else wants your money.

From 2001 to 2016, for active mutual funds, overall around 92% did not beat their respective indexes. The 8% that did beat their respective indexes were not the same ones each year, as those in the top 25% changed each year, such that 0% stayed in the top 25% after 5 years and 2% stayed in the top 50%, i.e., those that won in one year were not in the winner's circle 5 years later. The majority weren't in that circle 2 years after being in the top 25%, or 3 years, or 4 years, or up to 15 years.

These data are from 2001-2016. This is after the invention of the internet, after having more and more information at your fingertips for the cost of an internet connection. This is after databases and immediate access to information. We, as human beings and human beings using computers, don't appear to have figured out which stocks will go up and which will go down. I mean, hindsight is perfect, but predicting the future seems to be beyond us.[81]

Can you beat the market index in one year? Yes, many have. Can you do it consistently? Well, no one else has (some have won for 30 years straight only to lose all those gains, accumulated over the course of 30 years, within the next 5 years), but maybe you'll be the first; however, the odds are against any of us doing just that. It gets worse when you consider the extra costs, since the person on the other end has to get paid for their hard work (and pay their team for their hard work) and that decreases the overall return you can get as an investor.

For the record, I'm a passive investor with index funds. My inappropriately high opinion of myself does not extend to fields where I don't have the time to put in the work that people in the field do, and while the past is not the future, I don't think I can pick the winning mutual fund managers who will pick winning stocks consistently.

Fees and costs

Fees and costs are among the few things that you can control in investing, and they have significant effects on what happens to your investments. The effects of costs compound over time; similar to the principle of compound interest that was discussed under in the financial basics section, there are also compound costs.

---

[81] Well, except for Cassandra of Troy.

Your return on any investment is what the investment earns minus the costs.

Compound costs

So how do costs compound and what do I mean by this? I mean that over the time that you'll spend investing and saving for retirement, costs add up. So let's think about some costs that you might incur in your retirement savings for purchasing a mutual fund or the like:

1. Fund fees (listed in the description, can range from 0.07% to 2% or more of the total assets under management [AUM, aka the entire account])
2. Fund fees that may only be listed in the prospectus of the fund, including:
   a. Fees related to marketing the fund
   b. Fees for buying shares of something
   c. Fees for selling shares of something
   d. Fees for holding the fund at that particular company
   e. Fees for hiring specific managers
   f. Fees for record keeping
   g. Fees for accounting
   h. Fees for legal expenses
3. "Other fees" that are unspecified but may still be listed somewhere as being your responsibility

When you look at all of these together, some funds can cost as much as 2-5% of the entire account, *per year*. The good news is that any savings at all is actually increasing the likelihood that you'll be okay later, even if you're stuck with these high-fee funds. The better news is that there are low-cost options out there that can let you keep more of your invested money.

Keep in mind: your returns on any investment are what the investment earns minus the costs.

Perhaps some numbers will help illustrate the idea of compound costs. Let's look at $10,000 that grew at 8% per year for 30 years (I am assuming that you won't look at this until you're closer to 35; if you're saving in your 20s, great job!):

$10,000 growing at 8% per year for 30 years, with varying costs			
Starting Amount	Costs (as %)	Total in 30 Years	Difference from 0%
$10,000	0*	$100,626	$0
$10,000	0.1	$97,868	$2758
$10,000	0.25	$93,868	$6758
$10,000	0.5	$87,549	$13,077
$10,000	1	$76,122	$24,504
$10,000	2	$57,434	$43,192
$10,000	3	$43,219	$57,407
$10,000	4	$32,433	$68,193
$10,000	5	$24,272	$76,354

*I should note that there is absotively, posolutely no zero-fee method of investing in stocks, bonds, or real estate; everyone needs to pay their bills somehow.

So having 2% taken away in fees each year would cost you $43,192 over time; when all the costs are factored in, 2% is not an outlier. You're not likely to invest just $10,000 and walk away, but this gets the point across- compounding costs describe how a small percentage cost can grow in influence the longer you have an investment.

Note that these fees do not go away if your investment decreases in a year; those costs remain and you still have to pay the fees.

Taxes

Taxes are also a cost you should consider. There are multiple ways that you can invest that are tax-advantaged. If you're saving for retirement, you should save in tax-advantaged accounts first and then, when those are all full (if you make enough money to do so), you invest in accounts that can be taxed (aka 'taxable'). The reasoning behind this is that you will be taxed on your investments' interest at the top tax rate you are paying, e.g., if your income tax rate is 28%, then 28% of the interest that you receive is going to the government and will not generate additional interest or do anything for your retirement.

Saver's credit

If you are a US taxpayer but not a student, then you may qualify for a tax break called the saver's credit. Basically, if you contribute to retirement accounts and your annual income is less than $63,000 (married, filing your taxes together) or less than $31,500 (if you are single or married but filing your taxes separately), you can get a credit of up to $1000 for saving for retirement per person (in 2020; check the IRS website for the current numbers).

Note that the government sets brackets for how much of your retirement contribution would be a total credit, i.e., a single person making $21,251 to $32,500 in 2020 would get a maximum credit of 10% of what they put in, meaning if they put in $2000 into retirement funds, they would get a $200 credit.

With this tax credit, you're getting effectively paid by the government for saving your money for the future. There are worse ways to spend your money.

How much should I save toward retirement?

If you can, the goal is 15% of your pay (more if that makes you more comfortable) if you want to retire in 35 years or so. If you can start with just 3%, or 5%, or 10%, then do it- the sooner you get started, the better off you will be. If it takes you time to build up to 15%, then you will be left with a decision:

"Do I go crazy now (just start at 15%) or build up to saving 15%?"

Building up to 15% will decrease the size of your retirement fund in 30 years (unless you play catch-up later) compared to just stashing 15% now. You can calculate the amount pre-tax or post-tax; it will make a difference, but not enough of a difference that you should let that calculation stop you from starting to invest.

If you can live on much less than you make, saving more than 15% can decrease the amount of time before you can retire; one calculation pegs it at ~20 years of working if you can save 50% of your income per year. However, high savings rates are more feasible if you earn lots of money (if your lifestyle doesn't creep up, saving 50-75% of a $200,000 per year income is feasible in most of the country). The decision is yours but you can, in general, save more to try to reach retirement (and financial independence) sooner- this is a major crux of the Financial Independence, Retire Early (FIRE) movement.

Which accounts should I choose for retirement investing?

Generally, the order is:
1. Whatever tax-advantaged account your employer offers to get the match (if there's no match, ignore this step);
2. Above the match, if you still have money to save, put it in your IRA(s);[82]
3. If you got the match and your IRA is full for the year (i.e., you put in all $6000), you can put more into your 401(k)/403(b) if the investment options are good;
4. If you want to save yet more and can put it into a governmental 457(b), you can do so;
5. If you want to save yet more for healthcare expenses specifically, a HSA can be used;
6. Taxable accounts (savings accounts, CDs, taxable brokerage [read: investing] accounts).

The main thing to remember is that you can do a lot of planning and calculating to save as much in taxes as possible, but actually saving money and putting it away is going to help you more than the perfect calculation. Let's look at an example.

You have $10,000 and manage to figure out the best way to allocate everything and get a 9% return per year for 30 years (after paying your taxes). You will have $132,676 at the end of those 30

---

[82] IRAs are more flexible than company plans; the company plan was decided by the company, not you; in contrast, your IRA is wherever you want it to be and in whatever investments you can choose at that broker.

years. In contrast, let's say you are less efficient with the same money (only get a 7% return, paying 23% more of that return in taxes) but you are willing to put away an extra $100 per month. At the end of those 30 years, you would have...$197,410.

As another example, let's say that my advice sucks and you only get a 6% return per year (I can't believe that guy!) but still put away the extra $100 per month. You would have, at the end of 30 years...$157,996. If you put away the extra $100 per month, you would need to experience a 5.2% return per year to have $132,569, close to the amount you would have if you didn't add anything to your initial amount and got a 9% return.

The US total stock market average return ("real return," which means that it includes inflation) from 1950-2009 is around 7%. Because this is "real return," it means that this is both actually growing and keeping up with inflation.

Consistently saving and investing your income is the most important process in retirement investing.

How should I invest (aka asset allocation)?

The internet is full of advice about what you should invest in and how much you should invest in each thing (i.e., asset allocation). Generally, a company that you use for investing will have some sort of quiz or advice about this. You will be splitting your investments between, primarily, stocks (risky) and bonds (less risky). The idea is that over time you will convert more of your savings to bonds to make sure that you keep your money (plus the growth over time) if you happen to retire during a recession or depression.

How do you decide this? You have to determine how you feel about the risk of losing money in a given year. The following question is a good estimator:

- In general, are you more concerned about making money or more concerned about losing money?

Investing is risky. Your money is doing things with other people who may or may not use it wisely. If you err more on the side of "I need to make money," then you can have a more aggressive investment strategy (greater percentage of stocks than others). Alternatively, if you say "I better not lose money," then you should follow a more conservative strategy (greater percentage of bonds than others).

- Aggressive: 90% stocks/10% bonds
- Less aggressive: 80% stocks/20% bonds
- Less conservative: (your age - 10)% in bonds/the rest in stocks
- Conservative: (your age)% in bonds/the rest in stocks

For the stock portion, you can invest in US stocks, non-US stocks, emerging markets, specific markets (e.g., healthcare), and REITs (which are stocks in a very specific industry, real estate).

The US is a significant portion of the world's economy, and so if you live in the US you will likely be asked whether you want to invest internationally. I do; the US is over 30% of the world's economy, but it's not the only show on earth, so I also invest in international index funds and thus own shares of companies from all over the world. The advice for this varies, but as a US investor I invest 10-20% of the amount that I put into stocks into international stocks. Some people don't invest outside of the US; you need to decide for yourself what you want to do.

If you choose to invest in specific markets (sector funds), then limit the amount of your investment in those markets. For example, the tech sector looked good during the dot-com bubble and looked really terrible afterward, but the energy industry's fundamentals weren't affected by the dot-com crash.

Regarding alternative investments, the recommendations for how much you put into investments that aren't stocks or bonds vary from 5-15%. I know what real estate is and I understand how money is made there (though I understand that I don't know enough to start buying houses myself), but I don't see a way to make real money from bitcoin, for example, without finding someone else to buy it off me for more money (i.e., find a bigger sucker than me). The choice of what goes where and how much is up to you; remember that these decisions are up to you and your level of comfort.

The most important part of this section: this is about **your** level of comfort- not a parent's level of comfort, a friend's level of comfort, or the comfort level of the salesperson, but yours. If your investments freak you out, figure out what to change so that you sleep easily at night- you need a plan that you will follow through on that will still meet your goals. For example, if you need more bonds to sleep at night, increase your savings rate to compensate.

But what should I personally invest in?

There are likely a number of you that went here immediately instead of reading all the stuff above. So here's the answer:

Typically, a target date fund.

Really, most of us should. I am a numbers dork and there are things I like to do with my investments (read: tinkering that I'll likely regret in 20 years), but most of us should use a target date retirement fund (e.g., MarketingName 2055 or whatever year you're going to retire) that invests in index funds and has low costs. These funds automatically rebalance and become more conservative over time (i.e., the bond percentage grows as you get older), so that when you're closer to retirement, you've effectively 'locked in' your gains. Alternatively, if you have a certain stock/bond ratio that you want to keep forever, a balanced fund is a great alternative (once that keeps a specific ratio, like 60/40, forever) if it is based on index funds and has low costs (typically, these funds have expense ratios below 0.2% as of this writing).

If your eyes glazed over most of this chapter, use a target date fund.

If you're not interested in finance, use a target date fund.

If you don't want to be bothered to rebalance or adjust your investments once per year, use a target date fund.

If you're worried that you'll panic and sell something as soon as something goes wrong, use a target date fund and lose your password (or store it in a safe deposit box or something).

If you don't want to think about it, use a target date fund with low fees, put the money in there, set it and forget it. It should serve you well.

Conclusion

Well, you've made it this far and you hopefully know a little more than you did when you started. The goal of this book is that you're a little better able to manage your finances, keep your expenses low, and save for your future. I hope that with your newfound freedom, you can give generously and love generously without having financial worries and fears dragging you down. If this helps you feel more at peace about your finances in tumultuous times, then that's a pretty good outcome for a verified nobody like me.

If this helped you, please pay it forward and get a copy for someone who needs it. Us nobodies have to stick together.

Good luck, and thank you for reading.

www.ingramcontent.com/pod-product-compliance
Lightning Source LLC
Chambersburg PA
CBHW020510030426
42337CB00011B/314